Use Your Intelligence

Norman Sullivan is the author of *Road Test*, also a Fontana paperback. He is one of Britain's most experienced driving instructors and is the author of several books about driving. He has also compiled a number of crossword puzzle books.

Norman Sullivan

Use Your Intelligence

Drawings by David Woodroffe

Fontana Collins

First published in Fontana 1978
Second impression January 1982
Third impression March 1984
Fourth impression November 1985

Copyright © Norman Sullivan 1978

Made and printed in Great Britain by
William Collins Sons & Co. Ltd, Glasgow
Set in Linotype Times

CONDITIONS OF SALE: This book is sold subject
to the condition that it shall not, by way of
trade or otherwise, be lent, re-sold, hired out
or otherwise circulated without the publisher's
prior consent in any form of binding or
cover other than that in which it is published
and without a similar condition including this
condition being imposed on the subsequent
purchaser

Contents

Introduction 7

GROUP ONE (not difficult)
- Test 1   15
- Test 2   23
- Test 3   30
- Test 4   37
- Test 5   42
- Answers   49
- Ratings   60

GROUP TWO (fairly difficult)
- Test 1   65
- Test 2   70
- Test 3   77
- Test 4   83
- Test 5   88
- Answers   94
- Ratings   109

GROUP THREE (difficult)
- Test 1   113
- Test 2   118
- Test 3   124
- Test 4   129
- Answers   136
- Ratings   149

Final Ratings   151

Space for Notes   153

Introduction

The word 'intelligence' is bandied about more nowadays than ever before, especially as psychometrics (the measurement of mental capacities) plays such an important part in our modern life. Yet is is almost impossible to give an acceptable definition of 'intelligence'; many have been offered, only to be criticised as inadequate or inaccurate. And even if an ultimate definition were arrived at, 'intelligence' would not necessarily be a quality that could be accurately tested; nor would it be seen as a prerequisite for happy and valuable lives. These reservations about the nature of 'intelligence tests' should be borne in mind by anyone doing the tests in this book which I have compiled with no more serious purpose than to provide entertainment.

To what extent – if any – knowledge should be allowed to play a part in questions of the type in this book is a matter of some dissension. There is little doubt that learning does not in itself promote intelligence, though intelligence can assist learning. One who is intelligent, can assimilate facts readily, reason logically and quickly, has a ready understanding of what is being taught, and can get to the root of a problem without becoming side-tracked by diverting issues, is likely to learn – and thus acquire knowledge – more easily than one whose mentality cannot readily grasp fundamentals, whose mind wanders off the subject, and who is unable to absorb what is being taught.

Throughout these tests only eight per cent (24 points out of 300) are based on 'knowledge', and even then the knowledge required can reasonably be expected from those who have some recollection of what they have read or heard. These questions add interest and variety to the tests and at the same time offer some slight encouragement to those who *have* acquired the *soupçon* of knowledge required.

When answering questions in which a choice of answers is given, only one of which is correct, you should try to delve into the mind of the question-setter. Why has he chosen the 'distractor' answers? They would have no value if chosen at random. Also, read the question carefully, since sometimes one word in it can indicate what the inquisitor has in mind.

People sometimes quarrel with the correct answers, offering what (to them) are perfectly valid reasons why other answers can be equally correct. But a certain amount of licence must be allowed for, and the correct answer will be seen to have more in its favour than dubious and weak alternatives that are upheld by those who chose a different answer. For example, if the question were:

Which is the odd man out?

64
48
8
14

a perfectly acceptable answer would be '14' – because it is the only number that is not divisible by eight. It is clear that in choosing the other numbers the compiler has ensured that they all have something in common. It is also reasonable to say that those who answer '8' – being the only single digit – do not have such a strong case as those who reason that if three out of four items have something *outstanding* in common, then the 'odd man out' is the one that does not share that common factor.

Do not deliberately set out to find unusual answers that could satisfy the questions, as often the correct answer *is* the most obvious one. Moreover, as time is an important consideration in answering the questions – as will be explained later – unnecessary delay in searching for traps that do not exist or refusing to accept an answer because it appears to be too obvious can jeopardise your chances of answering more questions in the time allowed.

Problems in intelligence tests generally fall into various groups, each group designed to assess a different aspect of 'intelligence'. One person might be very clever at solving problems of a numerical nature but very weak at those demanding verbal skill. Another might excel at arranging shapes or designs into associated groups but be quite unable to apply reasoning and deduction to another type of problem. Some problems demand the ability to visualise the position of an object after its position has been moved several times, and a person able to apply his mind to this type of problem might find himself inadequate at solving problems that require the recognition of a regular sequence of terms.

Compilers are not altogether agreed as to the best way to arrange these tests. Some maintain that it is best to group together all problems of a similar nature, so that one set of questions is entirely devoted to those demanding verbal skill, another to those demanding numerical skill, another to those demanding spatial skill, and so on. The argument in favour of this is a very forceful one: that by so doing it is possible to assess more accurately the relative strength or weakness of a person; to pinpoint more precisely in what subjects he is weak and in what subjects he is strong. The only drawback to this is the monotony when working on the problems. To have to answer several successive questions, all on the same lines, such as distinguishing shapes or patterns, becomes tedious and monotonous to the solver.

By mixing the problems in fairly equal proportions so that throughout the tests there is a balanced sprinkling of problems that demand verbal skill, numerical skill, deductive reasoning, knowledge (if included) and spatial skill, the tests are more enjoyable to the solver, whose mind is thus free to range over a variety of subjects without becoming stagnated in one subject for a length of time. Of course, it is not so easy to assess the weak and the strong aspects of 'intelligence' under these conditions, and at the end only a general overall assessment can be made. There is, however, a certain 'reciprocal fairness' about this: points lost through verbal inadequacy may be balanced by points gained through spatial ability. Of course, when the subjects of the tests are mixed in this way the most conclusive result is obtained from a high *overall* score, implying good 'all-round intelligence'.

In these tests I have chosen to mix the problems, as the book is offered primarily for entertainment and amusement, though I hope it may also prove of benefit. I make no claim that after you have completed the tests you will be able to assess your 'IQ'. This would not only be presumptuous on my part, but quite impossible, since an 'IQ factor' must take into account certain facts about the persons concerned – not least being the chronological age – and those facts would be unknown to me. For the same reason, any assessment of results must be comparable in some way with results gained from others in approximately the same age group, similar background and environment, and of a known 'mental age'. What I have done instead is to give 'average' ratings, so that at the end you can compare your results with others'. These 'average' ratings have been collected by pre-testing other people of a deliberately mixed type and of greatly differing age groups.

Some people whom I tried to test freely admitted that they just could not understand these problems and did not know how to go about solving them. These I have had to exclude, though I am quite sure that had they persevered with a problem for a little while they would have seen what was involved, especially if they had started on the easy ones.

Most people by now have had some experience with this type of test, though it would be fairer to everybody if nobody had! Then everyone would start 'from scratch', as it were, whereas, in fact, there is no doubt that those who have met them before are at an advantage. And the more experience they have had with them, the greater the advantage is.

An important consideration that helps in intelligence assessment is the time factor involved. A human thought is incredibly fast, but it must first be triggered off. Just as a computer, though able to carry out its tasks with phenomenal speed, is impotent until it has been correctly programmed, so a thought can pass through the brain in a flash, *once it has been initiated*. Evidence of intelligence is that the solver can immediately understand how to proceed; instantly he perceives a suitable starting-point, and his brain, once stimulated, races ahead and leads him to the solution. For this reason, the time taken over the tests must be considered. Were it otherwise, and if everybody could take as long as they wished, there would be little validity in the tests, since, given enough time to think, most people would *eventually* come to the correct answer. They would be able to explore the wrong avenues for as long as they wished before reaching the conclusion that they were approaching the problem in the wrong way and must find another starting-point.

A time limit has been set for each test, and you should make a note of your starting-time. As soon as the time limit is reached you should not take into account any question answered thereafter. There will be no harm in continuing with them, so long as you do not record the results you attain beyond the time limit.

Another reason for setting these time limits is that I have

tried to encourage mental speed; by knowing that you only have a given time you should not spend too much of it on any one question. If at a loss, instead of wasting time pondering over that particular question, pass straight on to the next one, so as to complete as many as possible within the time allowed. If you then have time in hand you can return to the questions you have not previously answered. In any case, you will not know at this stage how many points any particular question merits, since the points will only be divulged when you check your answers later. A question that temporarily brings you to a halt may merit fewer points than others which you may be able to answer quite easily.

Remember that accuracy is more commendable than speed. A person who can give a correct answer in one minute rates better on mental speed than another who gives the correct answer in two minutes. But one who gives the correct answer in two minutes rates more highly than one who gives an incorrect answer in one minute. Try to reach a compromise with yourself: on the one hand do not dwell too long on questions you cannot immediately answer, and on the other hand be prepared to spend a little time mulling over a question in the hope that something will trigger off your mental processes – ensuring that you do not spend more time searching for this starting-point than the overall time limit allows.

Start each test with paper and pencil at the ready, and take a note of the time you start. At the end of that time, whether you have completed the test or not, stop work on that particular test. Do not at this stage check your answers or count your score (both the answers and the points earned will be found at the end of each *group* of tests). If you did not complete the test, carry on with the rest of the problems BUT DO NOT INCLUDE THEM WHEN YOU ESTIMATE YOUR SCORE. You may rest as long as you wish between the tests.

There are three groups of tests in this book, arranged in order of difficulty. The first group of five tests are not difficult, and are designed mainly to get you accustomed to this type of test. Many of the types of problem encountered will be met again later in the book, but they will be of a more difficult nature. It is hoped that the experience you gain when working on the easier ones will help you when you come to the difficult ones. The second group of five tests are more difficult, and the third group of four tests are difficult.

After completing each *group* of tests, check your answers

and count the points you have scored, retaining this record until you have finished all the tests in the book. At the end you will find final ratings based on your results in all the tests.

Do not be disappointed if, when you count your score in any particular test, your marks appear to be very low. First, you will not know at this stage whether they *are* low in comparison with results recorded by others. Secondly, if you score low marks on one test you may score high marks on another, since the proportion of problems on various subjects differs throughout the various groups.

To summarise all this:

1 *Have paper and pen or pencil ready first;*
2 *Take a note of the time you start each test, and finish as soon as the time limit is reached;*
3 *After completing each group of tests check your answers and count up your score, retaining the record until the end;*
4 *Do not be disappointed if you appear to have low scores;*
5 *If you have not completed a test by the end of the time limit, continue with the remaining problems, but do not count any points scored from them.*

Now all that remains is to hope you enjoy pitting your wits against all these problems and that you gain benefit from them.

All you have to do is to USE YOUR INTELLIGENCE!

Grays, Essex.   Norman Sullivan

Group one
(*not difficult*)

Test 1
Time limit: 20 minutes

1 Which of the numbered figures belongs to B?

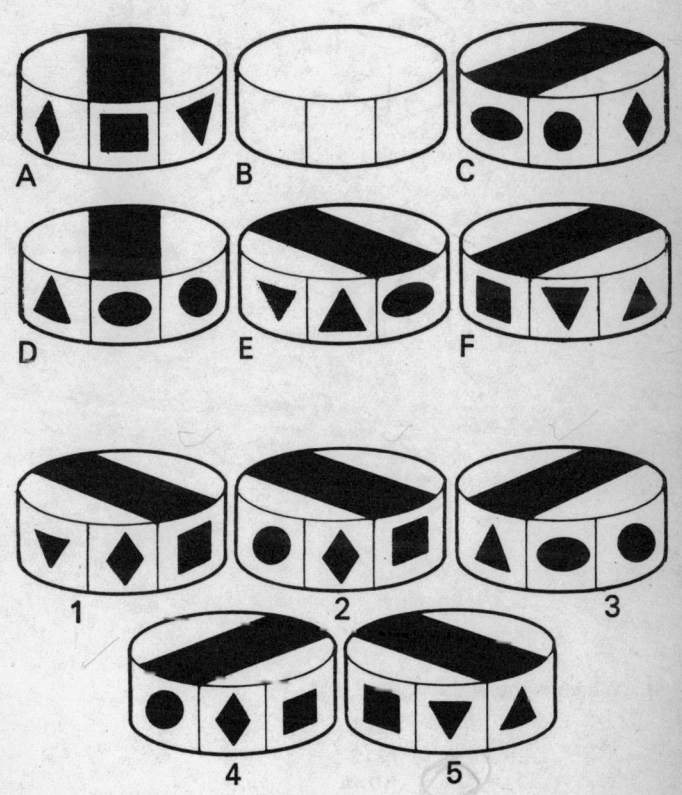

16 Group 1

2 Which is the odd word out?

> CHAFED
> AVONMOUTH
> COUPON
> HURSTPIERPOINT
> SHOUTS

3

If  = CAB

and  = FOE

then  =

4 Which is the odd one out?

> LILY
> IRIS
> ROSE
> DAISY
> ROSEMARY
> CARNATION

5 Which one three-lettered word, added to these letters, makes other words?

```
H - - - S T
M - - - Y
C O R - - - T
D R - - -
- - - R O U S
```

6

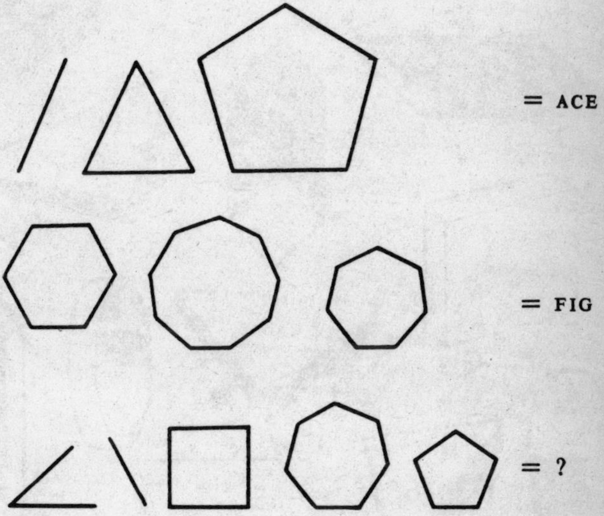

/ △ ⬠ = ACE

⬡ ◯ ⯂ = FIG

∠ ▢ ⯂ ⬠ = ?

18 Group 1

7 Which one is wrong?

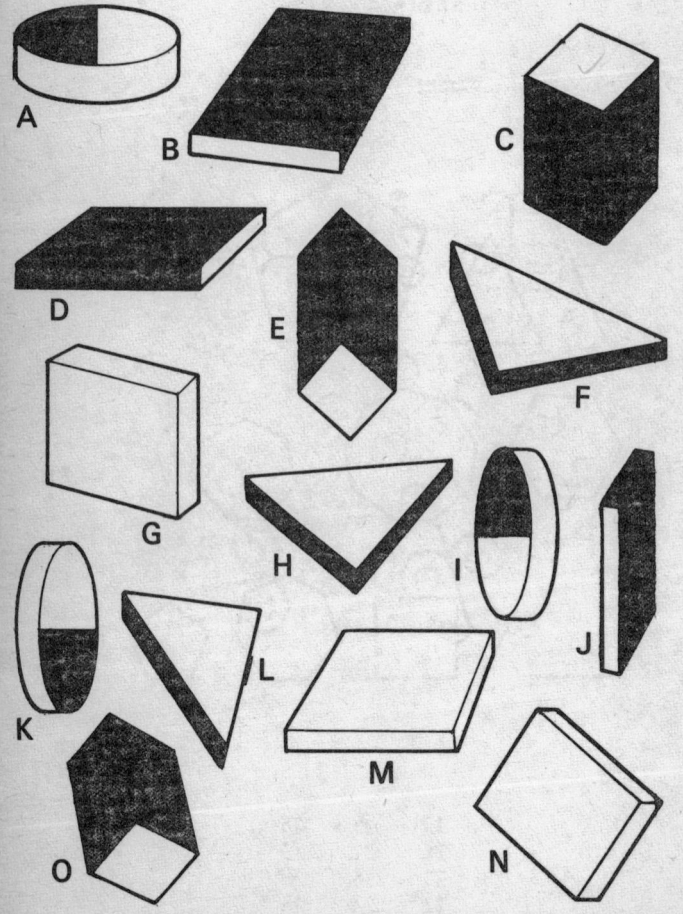

8 Which word does not conform with the others?

>   ANTICIPANT
>   PARAGRAPH
>   TINTINNABULATION
>   BEDAUBED
>   REDISCOVERED

9 Which one is different?

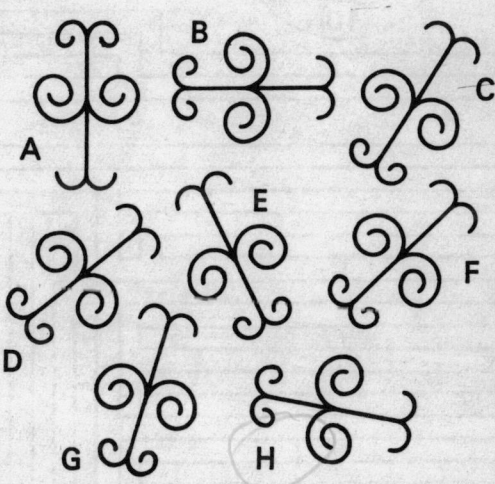

10 What is x?

17	33	25
36	11	15
21	16	x
12	22	34
14	18	10

20 Group 1

11 Using your eye only (not a pointer), which darts have scored 10, 25 and 50 respectively?

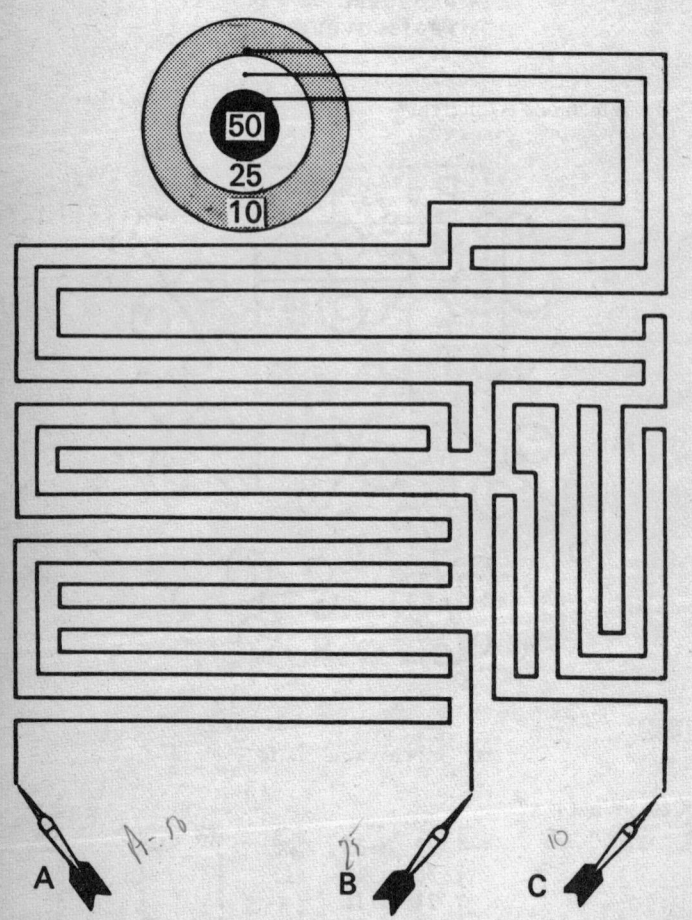

12 Pair each word in the first column with a corresponding word in the second column, finishing with five pairs of words.

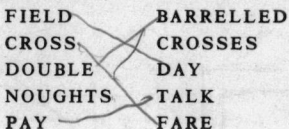

```
FIELD      BARRELLED
CROSS      CROSSES
DOUBLE     DAY
NOUGHTS    TALK
PAY        FARE
```

13 What are x and y?

E	A	4
H	E	13
Z	Q	9
T	E	25
K	F	5
L	J	x
G	A	y

14

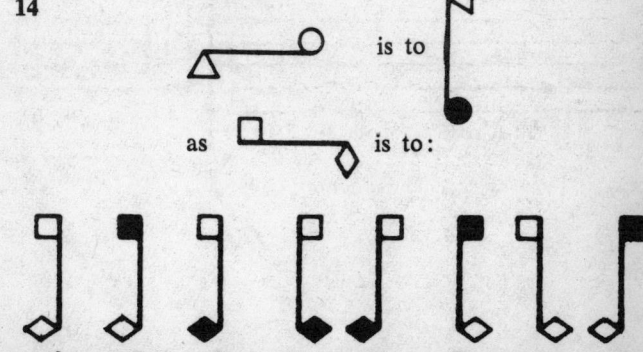

22 Group 1

15 If A were placed on top of B, which of the numbered outlines would result?

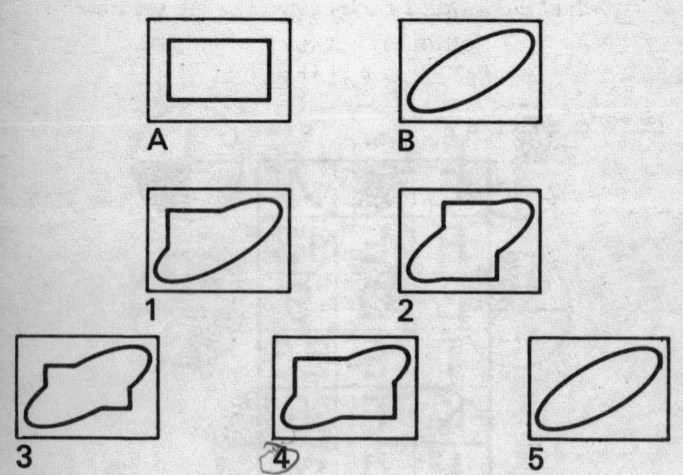

Test 2

Time limit: 25 minutes

1 Which of the labelled circles completes the sequence?

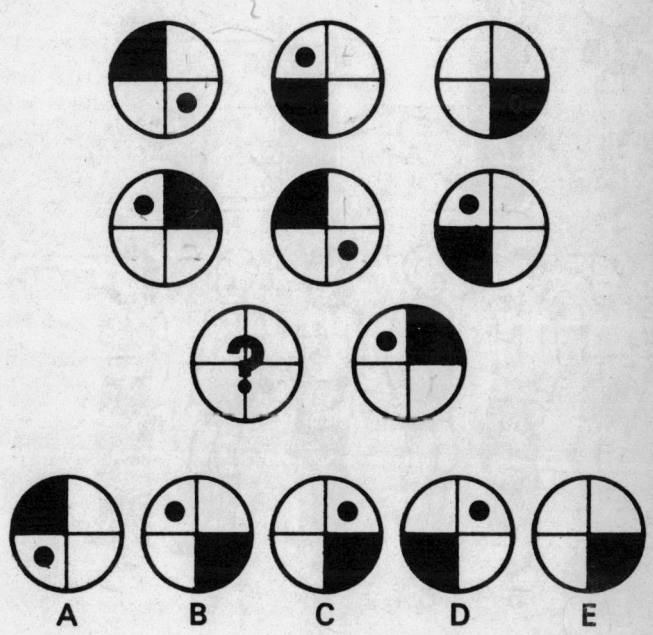

24 Group 1

2 Assuming that the top two boys are dressed correctly, which of the boys below are wrongly dressed?

3 Sixteen socks are mixed up in a drawer. Four are red; four are yellow; four are black; four are blue.

What is the least number you would have to select in the dark to be sure of getting:

       (a) One of each colour
       (b) A matching pair

Test 2 25

4 Which one of these is wrong?

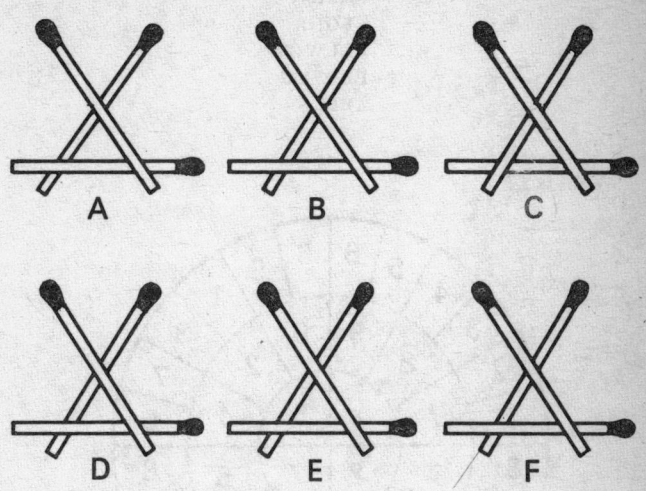

5 If you take B from A, which of the numbered figures remains?

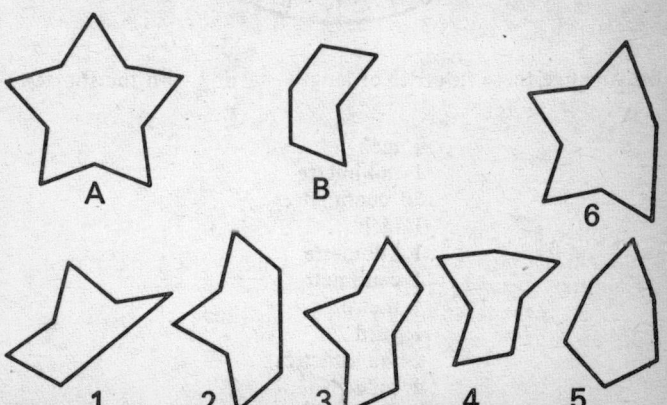

26 *Group 1*

6 Which is the odd man out?

> BNORW
> EEGNR
> ELLWOY
> ELPPRU
> AEELS

7 What is x?

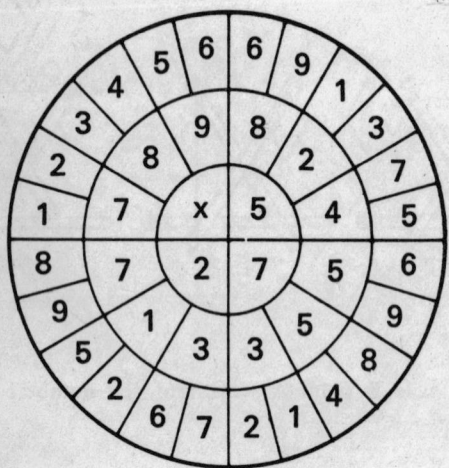

8 Arrange these in order of length, starting with the shortest.

> ¼ inch
> 1 millimetre
> 30 centimetres
> 1 inch
> 1 kilometre
> 1 centimetre
> 1 metre
> 1 yard
> 24 millimetres
> 1 mile
> 1 foot

Test 2 27

9 Which one is wrong?

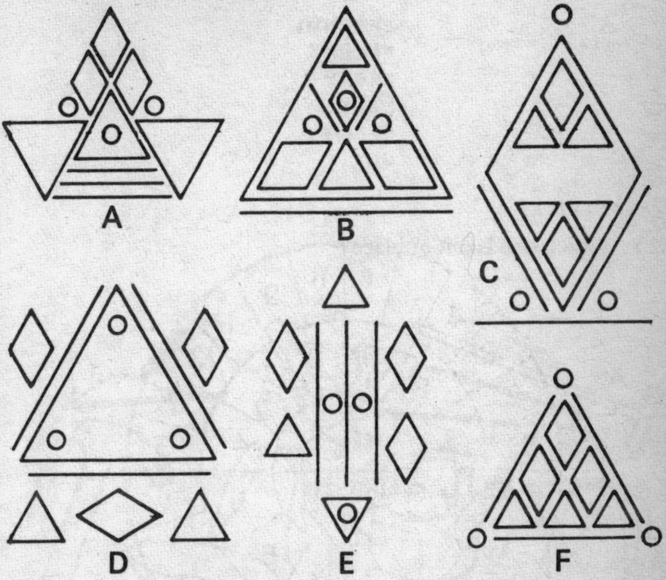

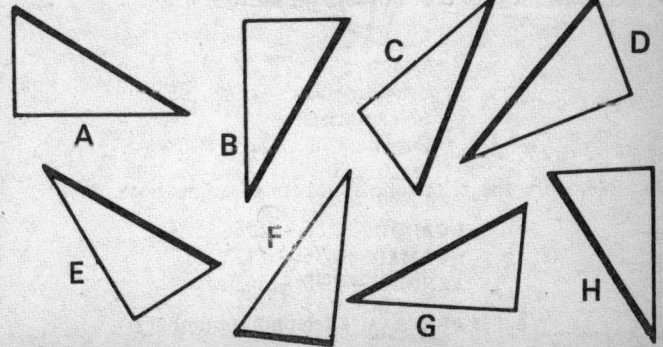

10 Which of these numbers – 182, 541, 360, 298, 433 – comes next in the sequence?

    123   412   323   513   631   ——

11 Which of these triangles is wrong?

28 Group 1

12 These words all have something in common. What is it?

> EFFENDI
> ELLEN
> ESSAY
> EXCEL
> SEEDY
> CUTIE

13 Which one is out of place?

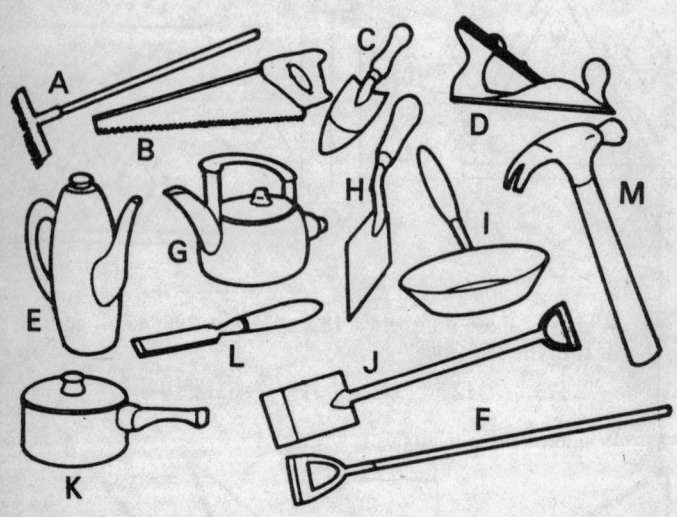

14 Here are the telephone numbers of some boys:

> ROBERT   86 – 5984
> NORMAN   36 – 8173
> ARNOLD   78 – 3620

What is BERTRAM's telephone number?

15 One of these is wrong. Which one?

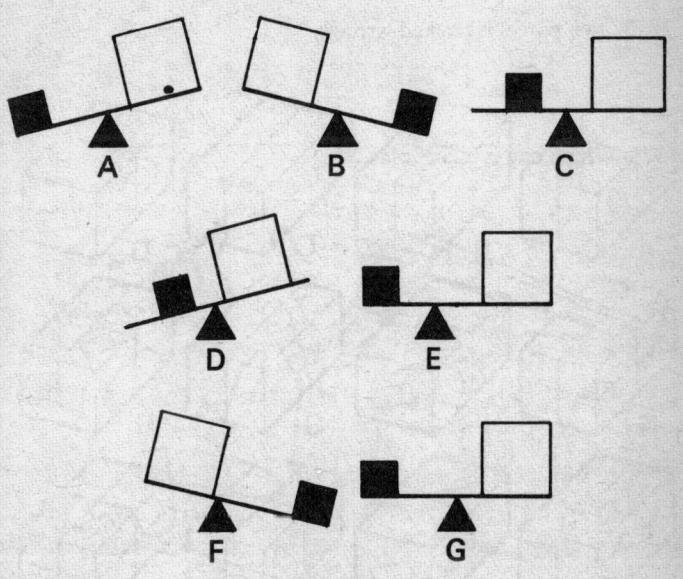

Test 3
Time limit: 20 minutes

1 Which parcel is packed wrongly?

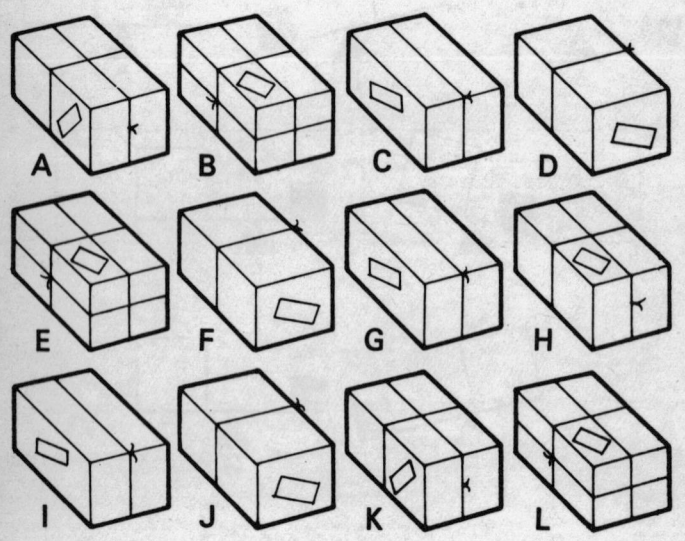

2 Which is the odd word out?

>STRAPS
>REWARD
>RENNET
>STROP
>STRAP
>DRAWS

3 Which of these well-known quotations is wrong?

In the spring a young man's fancy lightly turns to thoughts of love.	'Tis better to have loved and lost Than never to to have loved at all.
A	**B**
The ploughman homeward plods his weary way.	Hail to thee, blithe spirit! Bird thou never wert.
C	**D**

4 What letters go into the squares?

1	2	3	4	5	6	7

```
1 2 3 4 5 6 7    A military throw-away
1 2 5 4 6 3 7    Nobleman
5 4 1 3 2 7 6    Made to see red
6 7 2 5 4 1 3    Disturb
3 4 2 5 1 7 6    Made to see red
```

32 Group 1

5 A train is proceeding along this complicated railway system in the direction indicated by the arrow. The signalman, normally kept very busy, has collapsed in his box.

How many crossings and how many points will the train go over before it is derailed?

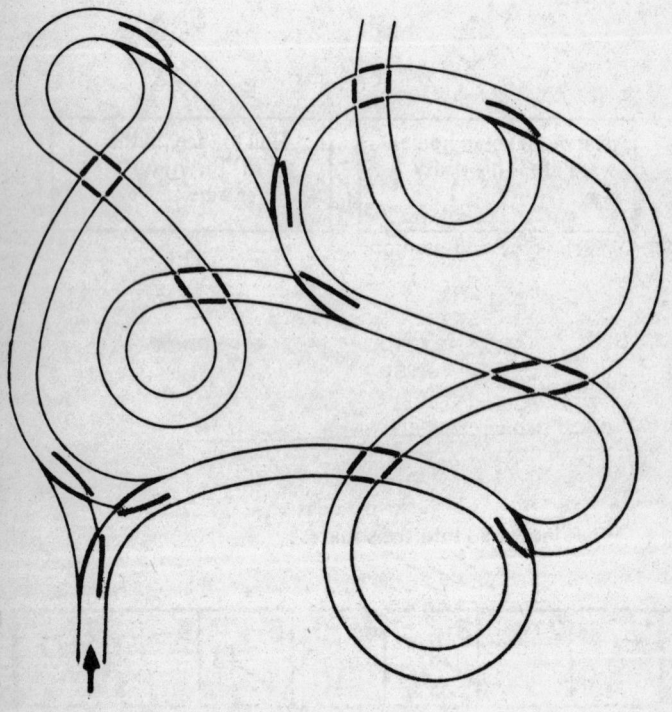

6 If MARE = REAM, what is RASP?

7 Which man is wrong?

8 Which is the odd man out?

DESCENT TROUBLESOME
CONFETTI PROPOUND
BANDANNA REMARKABLE
ENFRANCHISE

9 Which two of these are wrong?

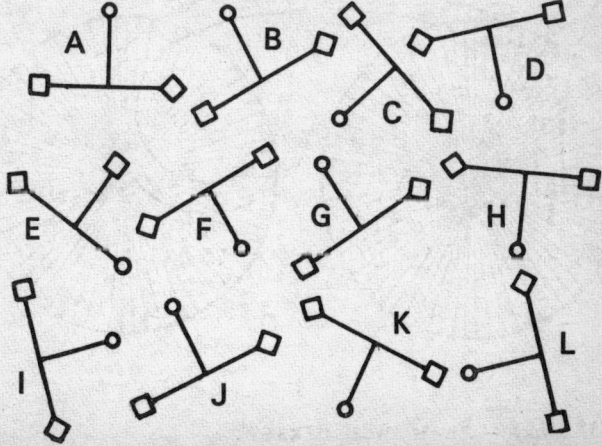

34 Group 1

10 Which words are spelt wrongly?

> HARRASSING
> ACOMMODATE
> SEPERATE
> EMBARASSING
> RECONNAISANCE
> SEIGE

11 Which wheel is different?

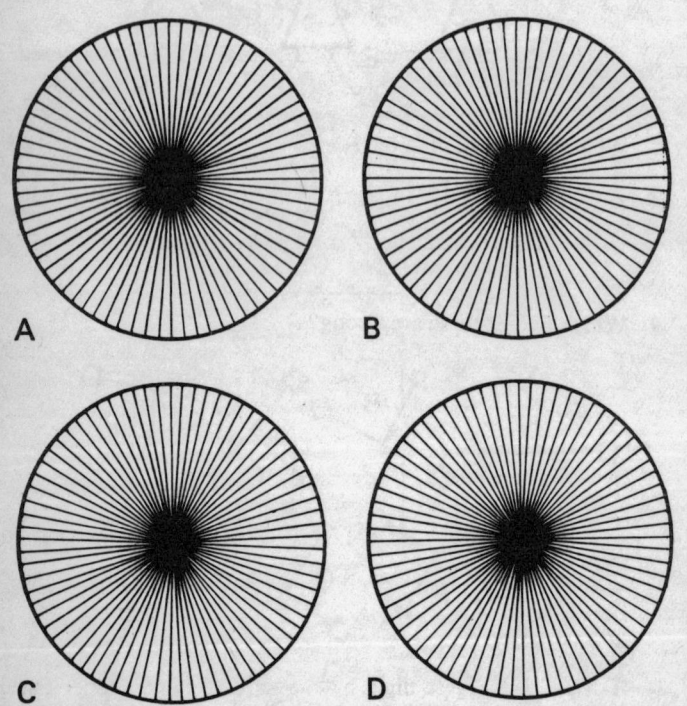

12 What letters are represented by x and y?

13 If A were placed on top of B which of the numbered outlines below would result?

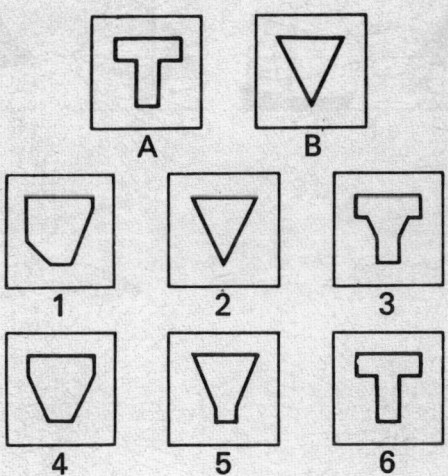

14 Divide the largest digit by the smallest and deduct the answer from the digit after the largest one:

      8 6 2 5 4

What number results?

36 Group 1

15 If the first four boats are correct, which of the labelled ones is wrong?

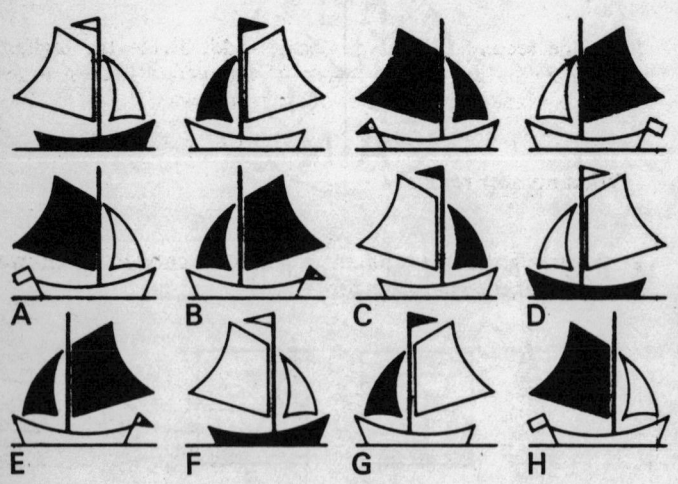

Test 4

Time limit: 20 minutes

1 If the second highest number is odd, divide the highest number by the second lowest. If the second highest number is even, multiply the two lowest numbers.

5 49 76 87 7 84 93 2 79 3 91 13 81 6 12 77 90 4

What number results?

2 Assuming that the top four churches are correct, which two of the labelled churches are wrong?

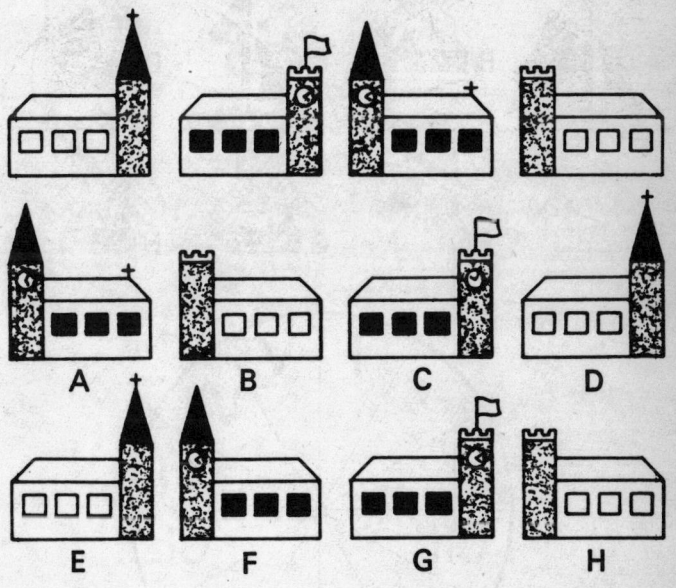

3 What two terms will complete this series?

A 2 D 6 G 10 J 14 — 18 P —

38 Group 1

4 80PQR = 6
9BD6 = 5
6890QDR = ?

5 Which numbers in the second column are associated with the words in the first column?

DIAMOND	40
RUBY	60
SILVER	50
GOLDEN	25

6 Which of these windmills is wrong?

7 What are x and y?

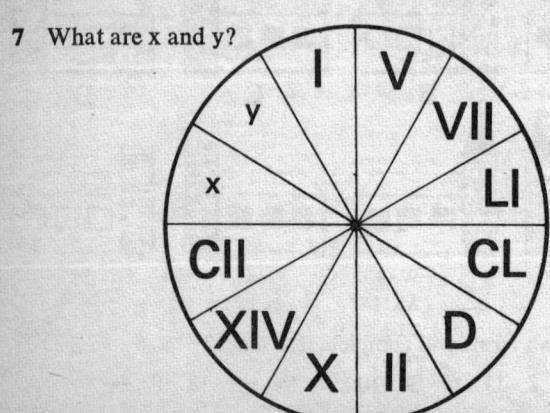

Test 4 39

8 Which is the odd one out?

> TITUS ANDRONICUS
> TROILUS AND CRESSIDA
> SAMSON AND DELILAH
> ANTHONY AND CLEOPATRA
> VENUS AND ADONIS

9 If STRIPE = PRIEST, what is RIPEST?

10 Arrange these patterns into four pairs.

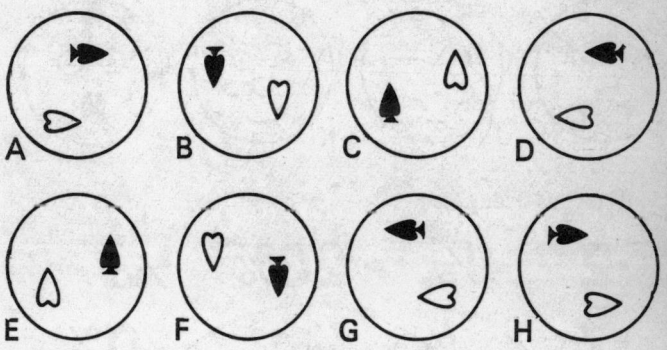

11 Which is the odd *one* out?

> LANDOR
> WARDED
> ARMY
> FLARED
> NICOL
> SINNED
> EGG-ROE

12 Who doesn't conform here?

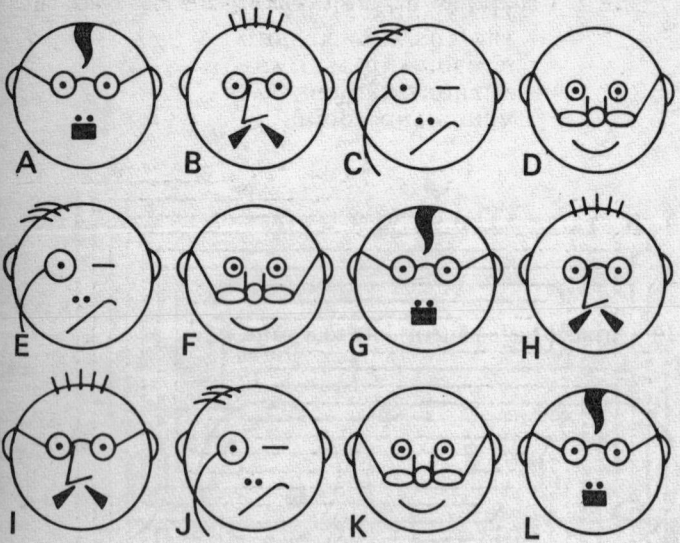

13 Which is wrong?

·2	⅕	20%	²⁄₁₀
·7	⁷⁷⁄₁₁₀	⁷⁄₁₀	70%
110%	¹¹⁄₁₀	1·1	1¹⁄₁₀
3½	3·5	305%	⁷⁄₂

14 Which is the odd man out?

BUTTERCUP   HYACINTH
GARDENIA   HYDRANGEA
GERANIUM   BEGONIA

Test 4 41

15 Using your eye only (not a pointer), and starting from the golf clubs (not the hole), which golfer has holed in one?

Test 5

Time limit: 25 minutes

1. Change CENT into DIME in four moves, changing one letter at a time.

2. Which pennon is wrong?

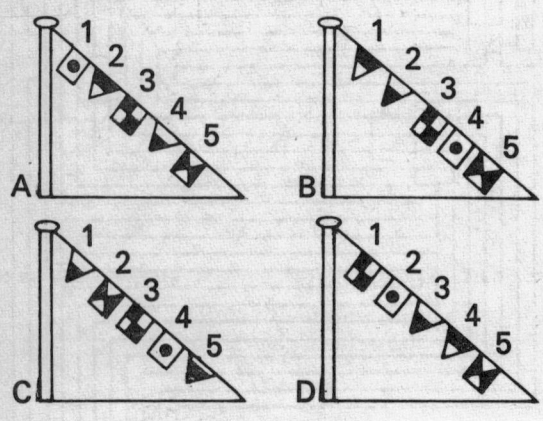

3. Pair the words in the first column with words in the second column so as to finish with five pairs.

        NEWS   FINGERS
        BUTTER   PAPER
        TEA   PRINT
        GREEN   LEAF
        FLY   CUP

4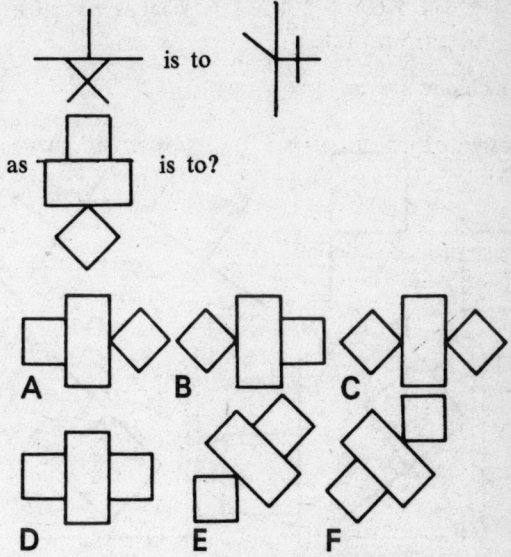

5 On a dartboard, which *four* adjacent numbers add up to:

(a) the lowest score;
(b) the highest score.

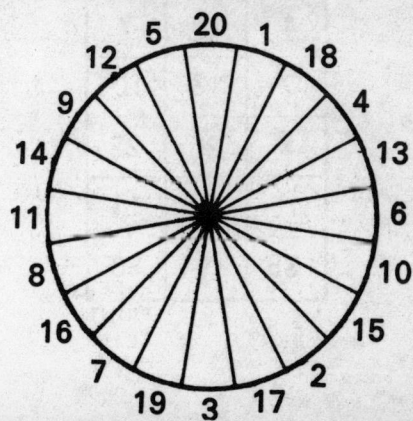

44 Group 1

6 If 1 2 3 4 5 6 = 5 2 4 3 1 6, what is EADNGR?

7 Which one is wrong?

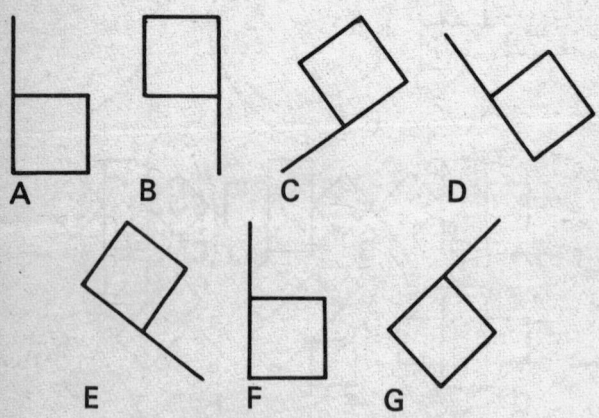

8 What are x and y?

4	10	7
7	13	10
x	25	22
11	17	14
35	y	38

9 Which cup spoils the service?

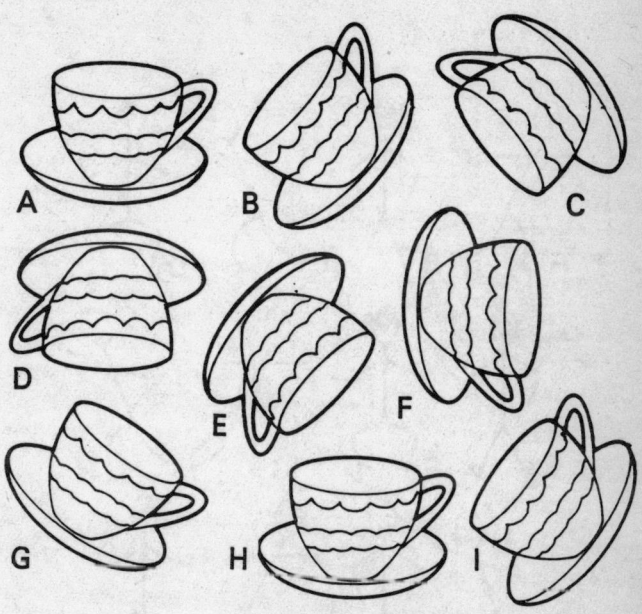

10 Which is the odd word out?

>   ABET
>   DEFT
>   MOST
>   FILM
>   PRAY
>   KNOW

46 Group 1

11 Which matchstick man does not conform?

12 Which one is wrong?

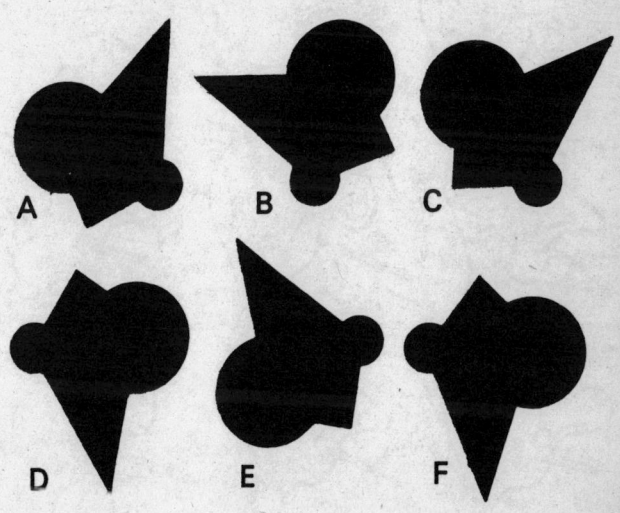

13 There are two countries mixed up in each of these phrases. What are they?

AN AIR-RIFLE, CAD
I'M A PERSIAN C.A.
CAP FOR LARGE NUT

48 Group 1

14 Which man has changed his appearance?

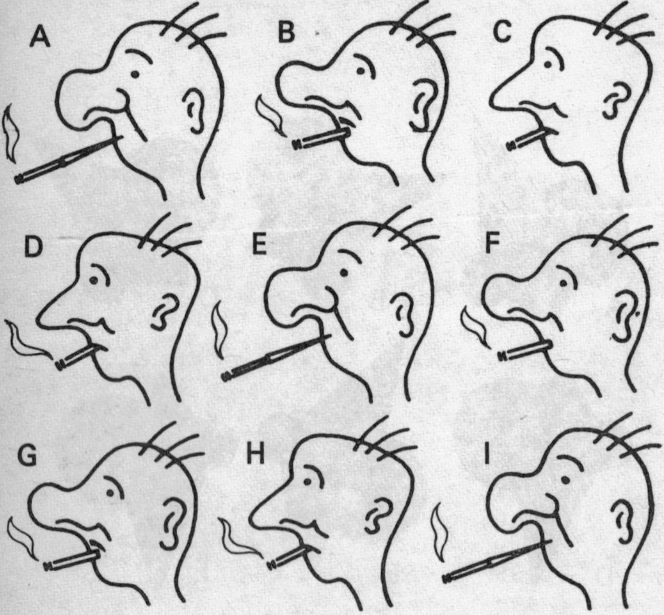

15 Which of these lines of symbols should come next?

Answers

Test 1

1 2 (*2 points*)
Examination of the top figures reveals that there are six different patterns, and from the manner in which these patterns change their positions it is clear that the figure is rotating in an anti-clockwise direction. The position of the black stripe on the top can be ascertained by tracing its movements through the other figures.

2 HURSTPIERPOINT (*2 points*)
This contains three consecutive letters – R, S and T *in their correct order*. The other words contain three consecutive letters *in reverse order*: chaFED; AvoNMouth; coupon and shouts.

3 BUD (*1 point*)
The left-hand face indicates the order in the alphabet of the first letter (B); the top face indicates the vowel following – A=1, E=2, I=3, O=4 and U=5; the right-hand face again indicates the order in the alphabet of the third letter (D).

4 CARNATION (*1 point*)
The others are not only names of flowers, but girls' names as well. 'Carnation' is not a girl's name.

5 ONE (*1 point*)
The words then become: HONEST, MONEY, CORONET, DRONE, ONEROUS.

6 BADGE (*1 point*)
The number of lines making up each figure represents the order in the alphabet of the respective letters. Thus in the first group, one line=A; three lines=C and five lines =E.

50 Group 1

7 J (*2 points*)
Discs are half-shaded on their faces; squares are not shaded either on their faces or their edges; triangles are shaded on their edges; rectangles are shaded along their *long* edges, whereas J – a rectangle – is shaded on its short edge.

8 PARAGRAPH (*2 points*)
The other words contain the same word twice: ANTiciPANT; TINTINnabulation; BEDaUBED and REDiscOVERED. 'Paragraph' contains the same word *reversed*: PARagraPH.

9 H (*2 points*)
The scrolls at the ends of the straight line are transposed.

10 16 (*1 point*)
Each column will then add up to 100.

11 C B A (*1 point* if *all* correct)
A has scored 50, B has scored 25, C has scored 10.

12 FIELD FARE, CROSS TALK, DOUBLE BARRELLED, NOUGHTS CROSSES, PAY DAY (*1 point* if *all* correct).
Proceed as follows: BARRELLED can only be paired with DOUBLE and therefore CROSS must be paired with TALK. NOUGHTS and CROSSES must go together, since DOUBLE has now already been used. FIELD could go with DAY or FARE, but, as PAY must pair with DAY, FIELD must pair with FARE.

13 $x = 22$, $y = 6$ (*2 points* if *both* correct)
Substitute for each letter its order in the alphabet. In the first line across subtract the second from the first to give the third: $E = 5$, less $A = 1$, giving 4 in the third column. In the second line across add the results: $H = 8$, plus $E = 5$, giving 13 in the third column. The procedure then alternates, first subtracting and then adding. In the sixth line, $L = 12$, plus $J = 10$, making $x = 22$. In the last line, $G = 7$, minus $A = 1$, making $y = 6$.

Answers 51

14 C (*1 point*)
The horizontal line becomes vertical; the symbol on the left of the line moves to the other side; the symbol on the right of the line remains on the same side but changes from white to black.

15 4 (*1 point*)

Test 2

1 E (*1 point*)
The black quarter rotates one move at a time anti-clockwise. The black dot alternates from opposite halves.

2 B, C and E (*1 point if* all *correct*)
Notice these points about the boy wearing short trousers: his shirt buttons appear on his left; his *left* stocking is down. As for the boy in long trousers, his sleeves are rolled up.

B is wrong because his sleeves are rolled down; C is wrong because the shirt buttons appear on the boy's right side; E is wrong because the boy's *right* stocking is rolled down. (This is the one you may have missed, as the boy has his back towards you.)

3 (*a*) 13; (*b*) 5 (*1 point if* both *correct*)
In the first twelve socks selected there could be four of each of three colours only; the thirteenth would ensure one of each colour. If four were selected they could be one of each colour, and only the fifth would ensure a matching pair.

4 C (*1 point*)
The horizontal match should be placed *over* the first match.

5 3 (*1 point*)

6 AEELS (*1 point*)
The others are anagrams of colours: BROWN, GREEN, YELLOW, PURPLE. (AEELS is an anagram of EASEL.)

52 Group 1

7 x = 5 (*2 points*)
The sum of the numbers in each quarter of the circle should be 50. In the top left-hand quarter the numbers as shown add up to 45, so that x must be 5.

8 1 millimetre, ¼ inch, 1 centimetre, 24 millimetres (2.4 centimetres), 1 inch (2.5 centimetres), 30 centimetres, 1 foot (30.4 centimetres), 1 yard, 1 metre (39.4 inches), 1 kilometre, 1 mile (1,609 metres) (*2 points if all* correct).

9 C (*2 points*)
Except for C, each figure is comprised of three straight lines, three triangles, three diamonds and three circles. In C there are three straight lines, three circles, three diamonds and *four* triangles.

10 182 (*2 points*)
The figures in the first number – 123 – add up to 6. The figures in the second number – 412 – add up to 7. The figures in the third number – 323 – add up to 8. The figures in the fourth number – 513 – add up to 9. The figures in the fifth number – 613 – add up to 10. Therefore, the figures in the next number should add up to 11, and 182 is the only number that satisfies this requirement.

11 F (*1 point*)
All are right-angled triangles, and the hypotenuse (the side opposite the right angle) is heavily shaded, except in F.

12 Phonetically, they can all be spelled by letters (*1 point*)
Effendi – F N D, Ellen – L N, essay – S A, excel – X L, seedy – C D, cutie – Q T.

13 H: a plasterer's trowel (*1 point*)
Other than this there are four gardening tools – A: rake, C: trowel, F: hoe and J: spade; four carpenter's tools – B: saw, D: plane, L: chisel and M: hammer; and four kitchen utensils – E: coffee pot, G: kettle, I: frying pan and K: saucepan.

14 59—84871 (*1 point*)
Numerals are substituted for letters, as is clear if the

Answers 53

first three names and numbers are examined carefully: B = 5 (B in Robert); E = 9 (E in Robert); R = 8 (R in Robert twice, in Norman and in Arnold). It is this repetition of letter with the same numeral substituted that indicates that a simple substitution is being used. T = 4 (T in Robert); R = 8 (already established); A = 7 (A in Arnold and also in Norman); M = 1 (M in Norman).

15 G (*1 point*)
By examining all the other balances it is obvious that the smaller weight (the black one) is the heavier. In G the two weights are equally spaced from the fulcrum and yet the scales balance – which, of course, could not happen.

Test 3

1 H (*1 point*)
The labels are affixed according to how the parcels are tied up. B, E and L are all the same; C, G and I are all the same; D, F and J are all the same. A, H and K *should* be all the same, except that the label is in the wrong place on parcel H.

2 STRAPS (*1 point*)
All the others make words when they are reversed: DRAWER, TENNER, PORTS, PARTS, SWARD. STRAPS does *not* make a word when it is reversed.

3 B (*1 point*)
If this defeated you it proves that the eye sees what it wants to see, and not what it *really* sees. The word 'to' has been repeated – 'Than never to *to* have loved at all.'

4

| ¹G | ²R | ³E | ⁴N | ⁵A | ⁶D | ⁷E |

(*2 points*)

54 *Group 1*

5 Five crossings and six points (*1 point* if *both* correct)

6 SPAR (*1 point*)
The letters of MARE have been transposed in the order: 3 4 2 1, and the letters of RASP must be transposed in the same order.

7 A (*1 point*)
All the other men are made up of three dots, one triangle, six straight lines and one circle. In A there are seven straight lines.

8 CONFETTI (*1 point*)
All the others contain a unit of currency: desCENT, bandANNA, enFRANchise, tROUBLEsome, proPOUND, reMARKable.

9 C and E (*1 point*)
There should be a circle at the end of the bisecting line, a rectangle on the left of the lower line and a diamond on the right.
In C the diamond and rectangle have changed places, and in E they have *all* changed places.

10 They are *all* spelt wrongly! (*1 point*, but *deduct 1 point* for each word you thought was right.)

11 C (*1 point*)
C has 73 spokes. All the other wheels have 72.

12 X = T; y = B (*1 point* if *both* correct)
The word is TRIBUNAL.

13 3 (*1 point*)

14 2 (*1 point*)
8 divided by 2 = 4, 6 minus 4 = 2.

15 B (*2 points*)
Yachts with white sails and a black hull fly a triangular white pennon from the masthead. Yachts with a black fore-sail and a white stern-sail have a white hull and fly a black pennon from the masthead.

Answers 55

Yachts with both sails black have a white hull and fly a triangular pennon at the stern. This pennon should be black in the pointed half.

B has the pointed half of the pennon white, and is, therefore, wrong.

Yachts with a white fore-sail and a black stern-sail have a white hull and fly a rectangular white flag from the stern.

Test 4

1 31 (*1 point*)
The highest number is 93, and the second highest is 91. The lowest number is 2, and the second lowest is 3. Therefore 93 is divided by 3, giving 31.

2 C and F (*1 point* if *both* correct)
Examination of the four churches on top reveals the following:
If there is a steeple on the right there is a cross on top of the steeple and the windows are white; if there is a steeple on the left there is a cross at the back of the church and the windows are black; if there is a tower on the right there is a flag flying from the top of the tower and the windows are black; if there is a tower on the left there is no flag at all and the windows are white; a church with a tower on the right has a clock showing approximately ten past four; a church with a steeple on the left has a clock showing the same time.
C is wrong because the clock shows the wrong time, and F is wrong because there is no cross at the back of the church and no clock.

3 M and 22 (*1 point* if *both* correct)
There are two sequences here. The letters miss two each time: A D G J M P; the numbers increase by four each time: 2 6 10 14 18 22.

Group 1

4 8 (*1 point*)
The number is the total of fully enclosed loops or rings in the letters. For example: 8 (two enclosed rings); O (one enclosed ring); P (one enclosed ring); Q (one enclosed ring); R (one enclosed loop) – total = 6.

5 These refer to wedding anniversaries.

DIAMOND	–	60 (years)
RUBY	–	40 (years)
SILVER	–	25 (years)
GOLDEN	–	50 (years)

(*1 point* if *all* correct)

6 G (*1 point*)
The sails are turning anti-clockwise The first movement is a quarter-turn (B); then two quarter-turns (C); then three quarter-turns (D), and so on. After F there should be *six* quarter-turns, so that the black sail in G should be at 11 o'clock instead of 1 o'clock.

7 x = CCC; y = M (*1 point* if *both* correct)
The higher numbers are double the opposite numbers throughout, expressed in Roman numerals. Thus:

II is opposite I
X is opposite V
XIV is opposite VII
CII is opposite LI
CCC is opposite CL
M is opposite D

8 SAMSON AND DELILAH (*1 point*)
All the others are titles of works by Shakespeare.

9 SPETRI (*1 point*)
The letters in the first word (STRIPE) have been transposed to the order: 5 3 4 6 1 2, so the letters of RIPEST must be transposed in the same way.

10 AF, BD, CH, EG (*2 points* if *all* correct)

11 ARMY (*2 points*)
ARMY is an anagram of Mary, which is a girl's name.

Answers 57

All the others are anagrams of boys' names: LANDOR – Ronald or Roland, WARDED – Edward, FLARED – Alfred, NICOL – Colin, SINNED – Dennis, EGG-ROE – George.

12 I (*1 point*)
I should be wearing *pince-nez*!

13 305% (*2 points*)
Other than this, each line expresses the same proportion in different ways. In the bottom line 3½ is the same as 3.5 or 7/2, but 305% is equivalent to 3.05.

14 BUTTERCUP (*1 point*)
A buttercup is a wild flower, whereas all the others are cultivated.

15 B (*1 point*)

Test 5

1 CENT – DENT – DINT – DINE – DIME (*1 point*)
(If you solved this with other words, score *1 point* provided all the words are genuine.)

2 C5 (*1 point*)
The triangular pennon half black and half white should be white on the pointed half.

3 NEWS   PRINT
   BUTTER CUP
   TEA   LEAF
   GREEN   FINGERS
   FLY   PAPER
(*3 points* if *all* correct. If you have paired GREEN with LEAF, BUTTER with FINGERS and TEA with CUP, score *2 points*)
PRINT must pair with NEWS, therefore FLY must pair with PAPER or LEAF; if with LEAF there is no word left to pair with PAPER, and so FLY must go with PAPER.

58 Group 1

If BUTTER is paired with FINGERS it would mean that GREEN would have to be paired with LEAF, and GREEN LEAF is an inferior pairing. Much better is the pairing of BUTTER with CUP, so that GREEN can then go with FINGERS, leaving TEA to be paired with LEAF.

4 B (*2 points*)
The centre line in the example changes from horizontal to vertical; therefore the centre rectangle must change in the same way. The choice now lies among A, B, C and D.

The lower symbol (a cross) changes in the example from a diagonal cross to an upright one – in other words, it moves through 45 degrees. The lower symbol – a diamond – must be moved in the same way, so it becomes a square on a horizontal base, narrowing the choice to B or D.

The upper symbol in the example is a line at right angles to the centre line and changes to a diagonal line. Therefore, the upper symbol (a square) must be changed into a diamond, and B is the only one that satisfies this.

5 (*a*) 4 13 6 10 (total 33), *and* 6 10 15 2 (total 33)
(*b*) 19 7 16 8 (total 50)
(*1 point* for *each* correct answer. Maximum: *3 points*)

6 GANDER (*1 point*)
The letters must be transposed in the same way as the numbers.

7 E (*1 point*)
If the long line is placed as a base line, the square should be on the *right*-hand side of it. In E the square is on the left-hand side.

8 x = 19, y = 41 (*1 point* if *both* correct)
The number in the left-hand vertical column is advanced by 6 to give the number in the centre column and that number decreases by 3 to give the number in the right-hand vertical column, the letters representing the numbers which fulfil these requirements.

9 E (*1 point*)
The centre band is upside-down.

Answers 59

10 PRAY (*2 points*)
In all the other words the letters are in alphabetical order.

11 M (*1 point*)
Comparing the back view of the gentleman with D, F and L, it can be seen that the arms should be pointing downwards instead of upwards.

12 B (*1 point*)

13 Africa and Ireland, America and Spain, Portugal and France (*1 point* for each correct *pair*. Maximum: *3 points*)

14 F (*1 point*)
He has used a razor!

15 A (*3 points*)
In B the first symbol in A – the circle – has been moved to the end. In C the first *two* symbols in B – the square and the upright triangle – have been moved to the end. In D the first *three* symbols in C – the rectangle, inverted triangle and circle – have been moved to the end.

Therefore, in the next move the first *four* symbols in D should be moved to the end, thus bringing the sequence back to A again.

Ratings

The total number of points obtainable was 100, divided as follows:

Test	Points
1	21
2	19
3	17
4	18
5	25

Knowledge, flexibility of thought and deductive reasoning accounted for 14 points.
Verbal skill accounted for 29 points.
Numerical skill accounted for 20 points.
Spatial skill accounted for 37 points.

Average score is exactly 50 out of 100, divided as follows:

Test	Points
1	9
2	8
3	12
4	10
5	11

If you have a high score it is possible that you are well equipped in all skills, particularly spatial discrimination. A low score implies that you are lacking in spatial skill, since 37 per cent of the points are scored under this heading.

75 – 100 Excellent. The next group of tests should not cause you undue difficulty as it seems that you are well adapted to these types of tests.

60 – 74 Very good.

45 – 59 Around the average rating. No doubt you would have done better given more time. Satisfactory, however.

30 – 44 Perhaps you should work through the tests again, referring to the answers at the same time, so that you acquire a better understanding of what lies behind the questions. Almost certainly you are not accustomed to this kind of test, and found yourself following the wrong train of thought. Try to get a better insight into them before going on to the next group. Although under average, there is no reason why you should not improve if you persevere.

Under 30   Poor, I'm afraid.

Group two
(*fairly difficult*)

Test 1

Time limit: 25 minutes

1 If TWO = RUM, what is KEG?

2 Which one is wrong?

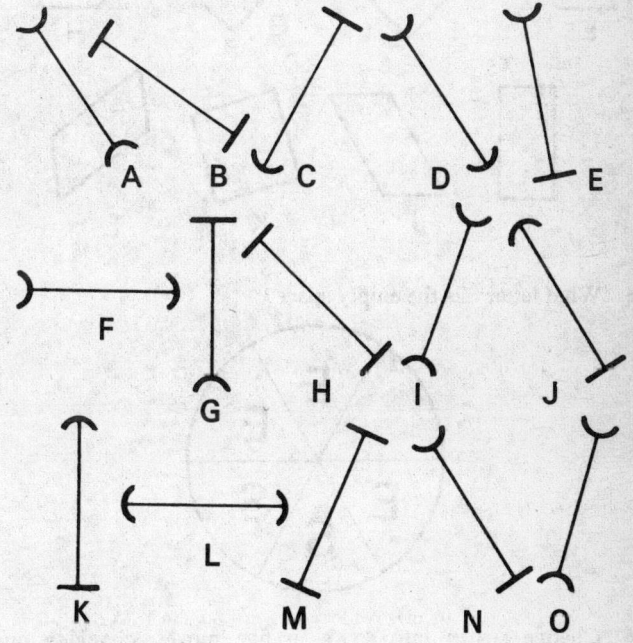

3 What are x and y?

    2 5 6 20 18 80 x 320 162 y 486

Group 2

4 Which of these is wrong?

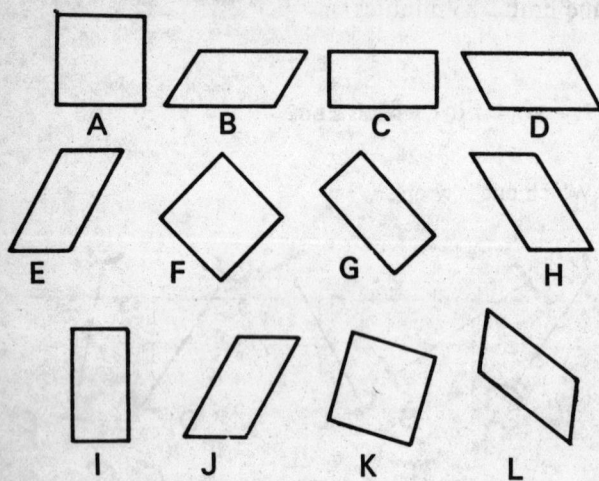

5 What letter fills the empty space?

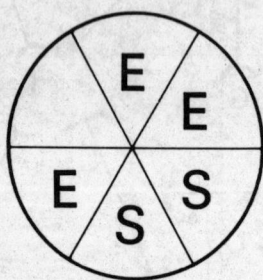

6 Change MOON into STAR in five moves, changing one letter at a time.

```
M O O N
_ _ _ _
_ _ _ _
_ _ _ _
_ _ _ _
S T A R
```

7 Which of the fractions in the second line continues the series in the first line?

$$\frac{84}{42} \quad \frac{176}{44} \quad \frac{104}{13} \quad \frac{112}{7} \quad \frac{416}{13}$$

$$\frac{95}{18} \quad \frac{318}{16} \quad \frac{227}{13} \quad \frac{308}{12} \quad \frac{704}{11}$$

8 Which of these cards are wrong?

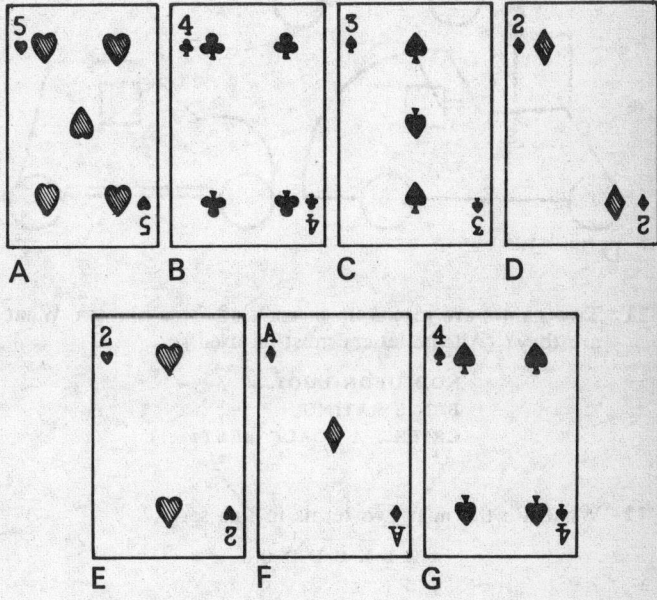

9 Find the word that means the same as the first definition and the opposite of the second.

STRONG POINT
PIANO

10 Which car has been wrongly assembled?

11 Two games are mixed up in each of these phrases. What are they? (All the letters must be used.)

>   NOD UPON LOOT
>   BEN'S RATING
>   CRIES: 'A BLACK BELT!'

12 What are the next two terms in this series?

>   A Z B X C U D Q _ _

13 Which is the odd one out?

>   ABDIILLRS
>   EKNOORS
>   ADGHRSTU
>   AABCGKMMNO
>   ADIOR

14 What are x and y?

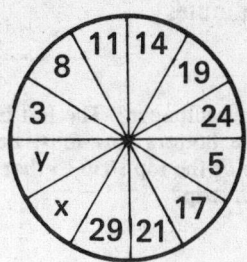

15 Which domino is missing from the set?

Test 2

Time limit: 35 minutes

1 Can you match wallpaper? The left-hand edge of one of the strips in the bottom row must be butted against the right-hand edge of the top strip so that the pattern matches perfectly. Which strip?

2 Which is the odd man out?

>   BEAR
>   FEAR
>   HEAR
>   TEAR
>   WEAR

3 Some words have different meanings which seem unrelated to each other. For example: 'skein' can mean 'a bundle of yarn' or 'a flock of geese'.

Give words to satisfy *each* of the two definitions below.

Musical instrument	Magistrate
State	Fast
End	Decide
Short	Instruct lawyer
Flag	Measure of timber
Glass	Acrobat
Round	Distributed advertisement
Receiver	Practise sword-play
Fence of bushes	Lay off bets
Keep out	Drinking-place

72 Group 2

4 Arrange these figures into six pairs.

5 Which fraction is the odd one out?

$$\frac{3}{5} \quad \frac{11}{13} \quad \frac{7}{23} \quad \frac{9}{16} \quad \frac{19}{29}$$

6 What are x, y and z?

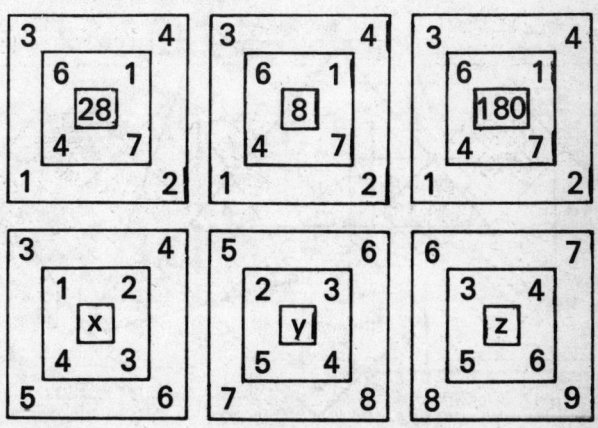

7 Find words to satisfy the definitions. Each word must contain an article of clothing.

> Pirate
> Cushion
> Blockade
> He's in hospital
> Incessant talk
> Part of clock
> Coloured arch

8 What are x and y?

    1 2 3 4 9 8 27 16 81 32 x y

74 Group 2

9 Which is the odd one out?

> RUN ALBUM
> COSY MARE
> LOVE IT
> THEN CUTS

10 Give values for x, y and z.

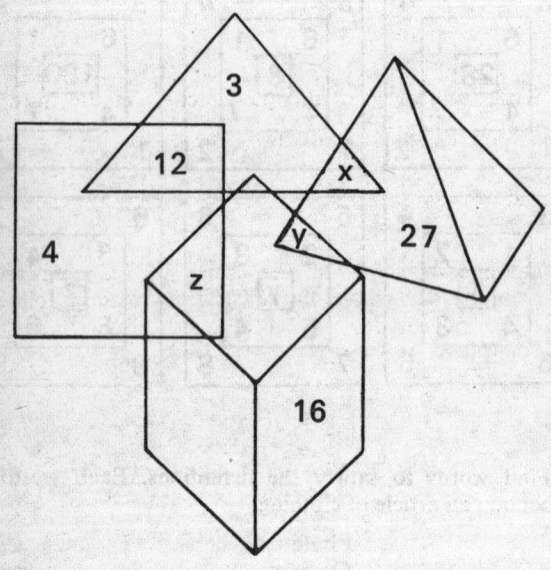

11 Which is the odd man out?

> BULLY OFF
> PAS DE DEUX
> CHUKKA
> THROW IN
> DEUCE
> COVER POINT

12 What word goes into the brackets to complete the first word. The same word *reversed* will start the second word.

POLE( )IT

13 Which is the odd man out?

CAPRIOLE
MARY
JUNKET
JUICY

14 What number goes into the brackets in the third line?

LEG (8) ARM
TOE (5) EYE
EAR ( ) LIP

15 Dominoes again! In the game of 'running-out' the dominoes are placed together side by side as follows:

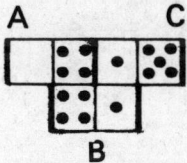

Assume that the first player laid A. The next player has to play one which will match *either* end of the one already played. Here he laid B – to match the 4; alternatively he could have played a blank to match the previous blank. The next player must play a domino either with one spot on one half to match the exposed spot on the 4/1 domino or one with a blank to match the blank at the end of the 4/0 domino. He played C, matching the 1. To continue the game it will be necessary to play either a 5 or a blank.

76 Group 2

Now study the game below. There is one domino missing. Could this missing domino be played at x or y or neither?

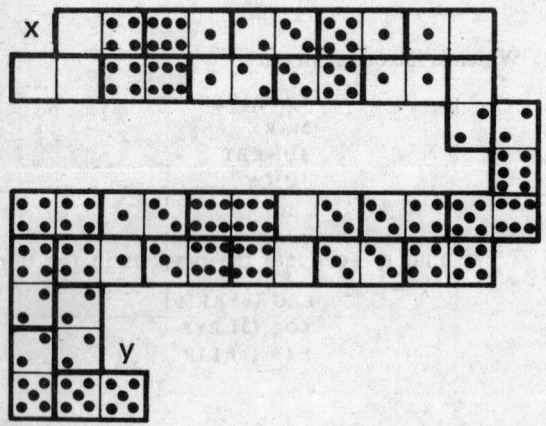

Test 3

Time limit: 35 minutes

1 What is x?

5	6	7	8	9	15
3	1	4	5	9	5
2	2	6	3	8	5
1	9	0	6	2	9
4	3	0	1	1	x

2 Who is the odd character out?

> MRS MALAPROP
> MR TAPPERTIT
> MRS JELLYBY
> SAM WELLER
> MRS GUMMIDGE
> JOE GARGERY

3 What three-lettered word added to each of these letters will make a four-lettered word?

B ___   P ___
C ___   S ___
F ___   T ___
G ___   W ___
L ___   Y ___
M ___

77

78 Group 2

4 PONY is to POUND as MONKEY is to:

> £5
> £10
> £20
> £25
> £50

5 Which is the odd man out?

> LONDON
> MELBOURNE
> TOKYO
> LISBON
> DELHI
> PARIS

6 What is x?

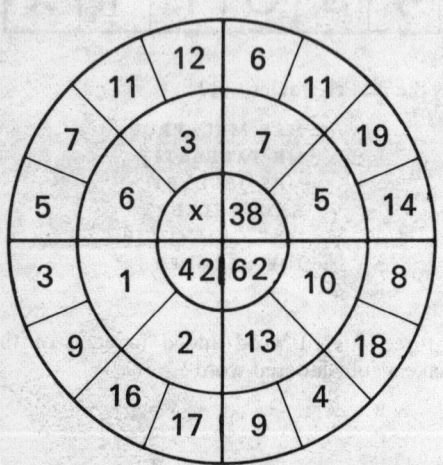

7 Join these syllables to make five separate words.

> ROT
> OR
> TER
> TRI
> TRY
> PEN
> GAN
> PAN
> TON
> TEN
> CAR

8 Which one is wrong?

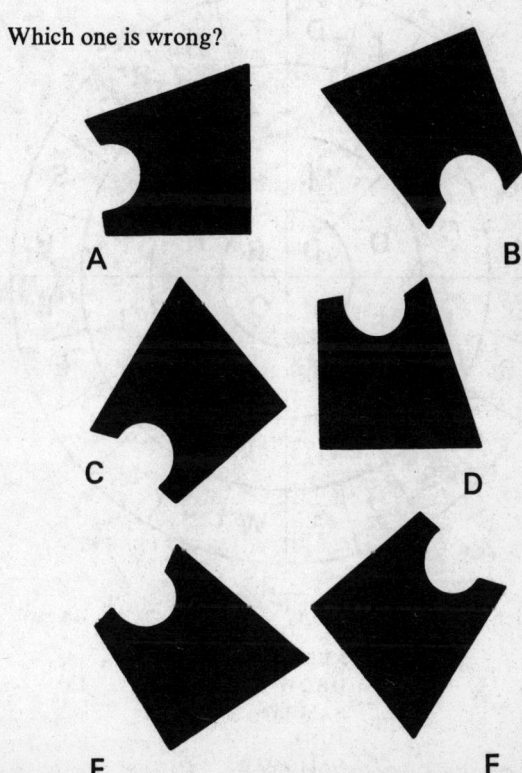

Group 2

9 Complete these words, for which definitions are given.

```
A R T - - - - - -   Edible plant (from Jerusalem?)
- A R T - - - - -   Division
- - A R T - - - -   Chest pain
- - - A R T - - -   Frustrating
- - - - A R T - -   Began again
- - - - - A R T -   For men only
- - - - - - A R T   Was it upset by G.B.S.?
```

10 Complete 1, 2, 3, 4, 5 and 6.

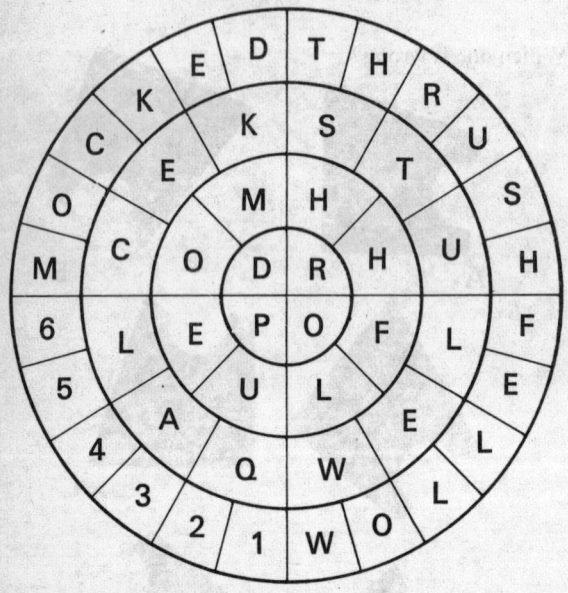

11 Which is the odd man out?

XEBEC
DHOW
SAMPAN
JUNK
SAMOVAR

Test 3 81

12 Why does the number in italics spoil this?

```
6 3 7 3 1
1 5 1 9 4
8 2 4 2 4
4 5 1 1 9
1 5 7 5 (2)
```

13 If 35 squared is more than 1,220, add the largest and smallest numbers together and give the result. If 35 squared is less than 1,220, subtract the smallest number from the largest and give the result.

17 5 15 8 18 7 16 4 13 3 15 5 11 6
12 4 17 4 10 7

14 Here is a game of snakes and ladders. If a throw lands on the bottom of a ladder you move to the top of the ladder. If a throw lands on the head of a snake you go back to the tail of the snake.

These are the throws from the die:

2 3 5 3 1 3 6

What word results?

24	23	22	21	20	19
13	14	15	16	17	18
12	11	10	9	8	7
1	2	3	4	5	6

82 Group 2

15 These dates have one thing in common. What is it?

>1147
>1534
>1786
>1903

Test 4

Time limit: 45 minutes

1 Which of the numbered figures belong to A, B and C?

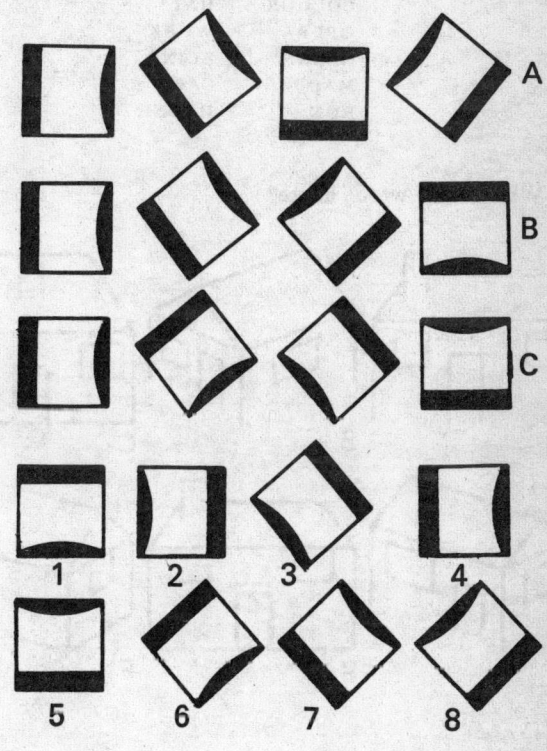

84 Group 2

2 Pair words in the first column with words in the second column, finishing with ten pairs of words.

BLACK	MAID
HOUSE	DIAL
CLOCK	BOX
STRAW	MADE
HOME	BERRY
COLOUR	HAT
OPERA	WORK
GLASS	BLIND
MAD	CAP
SUN	HOUSE

3 Which is the wrong house?

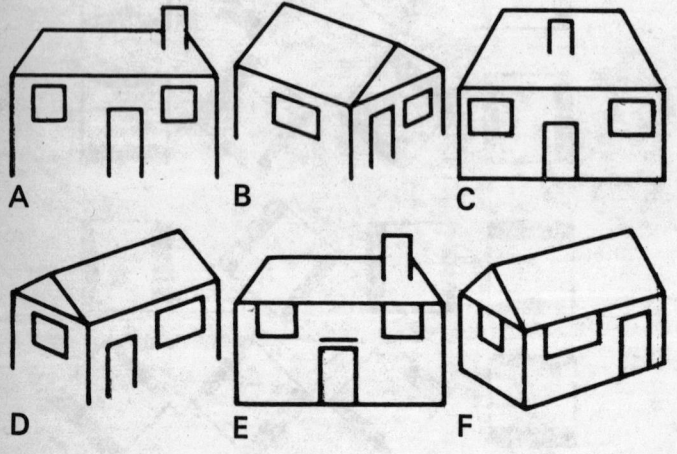

4 Starting with ERMINE, choose *nine* other words from the list. The first two letters of each word must be the same as the last two letters of the previous word. The final word must end with the first two letters of ERMINE.

Test 4 85

There will be three words not used. What are those three words?

ERMINE	ALTERNATE
ARSENIC	SOBER
ALSO	TENSION
EDUCATE	ARSON
NEUTRAL	ICED
ONAGER	CEDAR
SOLACE	

5 4735ℓ21 is to 359ℓ147 as MOTFᴲZU is to ?

6 Which is the odd man out?

> GRILSE
> PARR
> ELVER
> SALMON

7 Which one does not conform?

86 Group 2

8 Which word in the bottom column comes next in this series?

> FIX LIE TAN TEA WET
>
> NEW
> LET
> TIE
> WAY
> EVE
> WHY

9 Give words to satisfy the definitions below. Each word must start with the last *four* letters of the previous word *reversed*, and the definitions are *not* in the correct order.

> Startled
> Military mention
> Letter ornament
> Puzzling
> Wants
> It has burning missions

10 What numbers are represented by C, A and T?

$$\begin{array}{ccc} A & T & 1 \\ 2 & 0 & 4 \\ 1 & 1 & C \\ \hline C & A & T \end{array}$$

11 Which is the odd man out?

> SCAPULA
> SPATULA
> PATELLA
> STERNUM
> CLAVICLE

12 Place a word in the brackets which will complete the first word and start the second word.

BAR(   )AN

13 How many extra lines are required to join each letter?

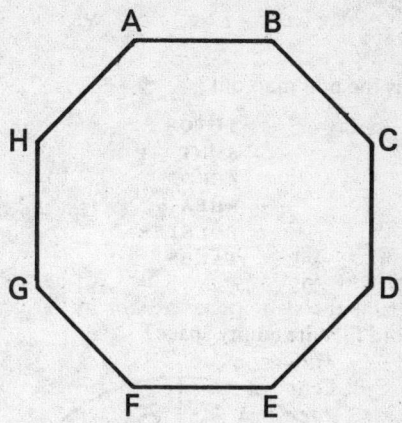

14 What word completes the fourth column?

183	153	167	193
122	233	176	172
DIE	CAD	BEG	

15 Which is the odd man out?

    GRIMALKIN
    SAMOYED
    CHIHUAHUA
    POMERANIAN
    BORZOI

Test 5

Time limit: 35 minutes

1. Which is the odd man out?

    TUTOR
    AUNT
    ACED
    RHEA
    BOLSTER
    TAKES

2. What word fills the empty space?

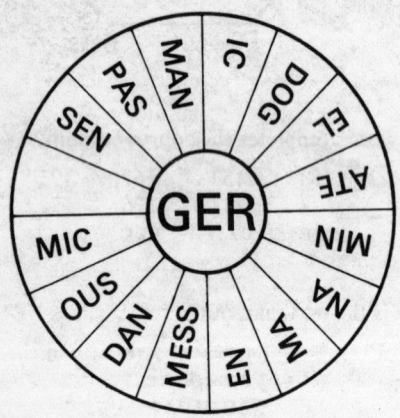

3. Unscramble these and find out which one is not 'mechanised'.

    TOM IS ROT
    FILM TAN
    SPEED TRAIN
    IN RIVER DART
    LOP IT
    TRIM? COSY CLOT

4 Can you mend a broken heart? Which *three* of the labelled pieces will make the heart complete?

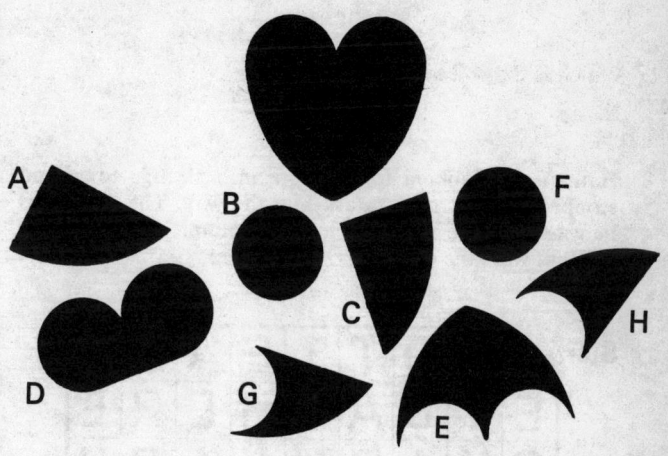

5 Here are three postal codes:

    IF14 4NM   (Hendon)
    JM6 15QC   (Ilford)
    TJ4 3TO   (Sidcup)

What is the postal code for Merton?

6 What letter is missing here?

90 Group 2

7 Which is the odd man out?

> CART
> MORRIS
> FERRIS
> POTTER'S
> CATHERINE

8 A man was looking for a house in a strange town and stopped another man to ask him the way. The directions he was given are contained in the diagram.

What were the directions?

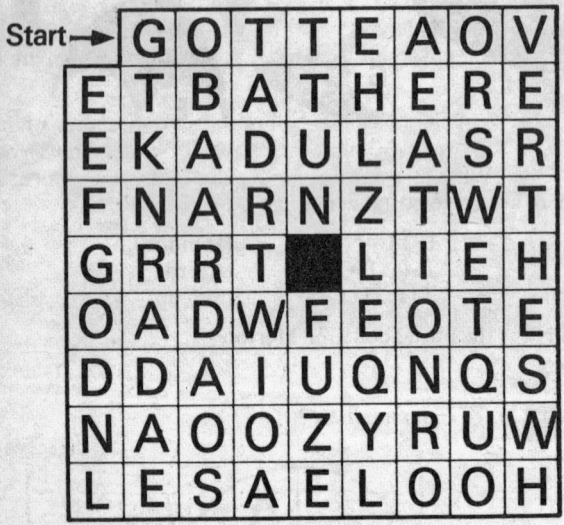

9 What are the next two terms in this series?

3 3 4 8 5 15 6 24 7 35 8 48 9 63 – –

10 Three dice are thrown simultaneously and appear as shown below.

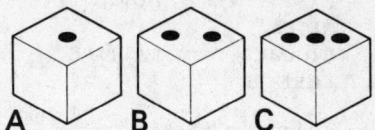

With each subsequent throw:

    A advances one spot
    B advances two spots
    C advances five spots.

(If a throw brings the total to more than 6, carry it over, thus: advancing five spots after a 4 would total 9, and so there would be 3 on top − 6 + 3. When, however, a six *finishes* on top, the next throw starts again at one spot.)

  (*a*) Will the three dice show the same number of spots on top at any time, and, if so, in how many throws?
  (*b*) Will the three dice all show a six on top at the same time, and, if so, in how many throws?

11 What are x and y?

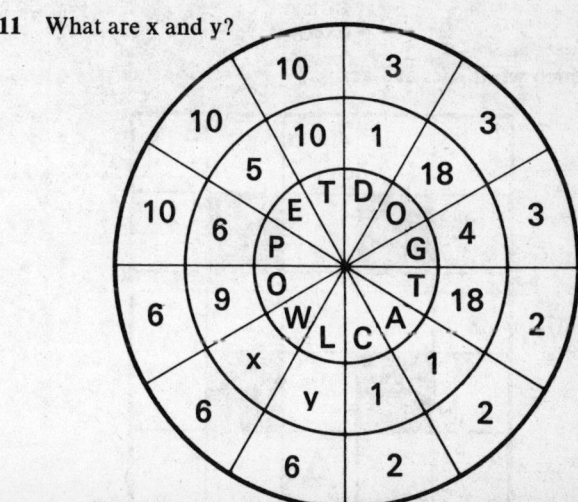

92 Group 2

12 Which is the odd man out?

    CASEMENT   DORIC
    ORIEL   BAY
    DORMER   LATTICE
    FRENCH

13 What word goes into the brackets?

    12 (PIG) 35
    20 (YAK) 18
    6 (   ) 45

14 Here is a miniature crossword puzzle. The words to be filled in must be chosen from this list:

    CAMEL
    LIMIT
    COMET
    YACHT
    MERIT
    MIMIC
    TOAST
    MAMBA
    LUCKY
    COMMA

Which word goes at 1 across?

15 What is x?

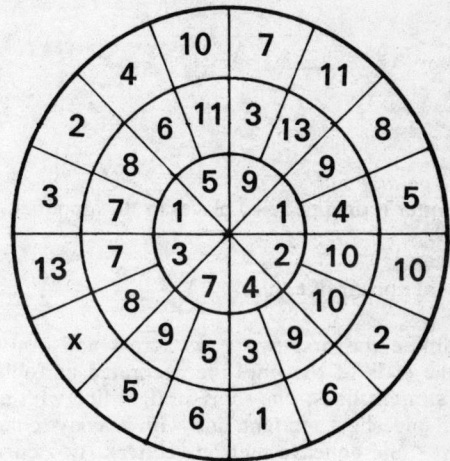

Answers

Test 1

1 ICE (*2 points*)
Each letter is dropped *two* places in the alphabet.

2 L (*1 point*)
It should appear like this:)————)

Examine the first two rows across and you will find that the ends of the lines are decorated as follows: two short straight lines; one short straight line with a concave curve; one short straight line with a convex curve; two curves – one concave and one convex; two curves (both the same.) L should agree with D and F.

3 x = 54, y = 1,280 (*1 point*)
There are two alternate series. The first (beginning with 2) multiplies by three each time – 2, 6, 18, *54*, 162 and 486. The second (beginning with 5) multiplies by four each time – 5, 20, 80, 320, *1,280*.

4 J *or* L (*1 point* for *either*)
Each row across should contain: one square; one rectangle; one 4-sided figure *sloping to the right* and one 4-sided figure *sloping to the left*. Consequently, either J should slope to the right or L should slope to the right.

5 L (*1 point*)
The word is: LESSEE.

6 MOON, MOAN, ROAN, ROAR, SOAR, STAR (*1 point.* You may have chosen different words, but provided the words are genuine and you have made the required number of moves, score *1 point*).

Answers 95

7 $\dfrac{704}{11}$ (*2 points*)

The fractions in the top line resolve themselves into this series: 2 4 8 16 32. To continue the series, therefore, the next number must be 64, and this fraction resolves into that number.

8 A, C, D and E (*1 point* if *all* correct)
They should be as follows:

9 Forte (*1 point*)

10 A (*1 point*)
The cars should be constructed with: five straight lines, one square, one curve and two circles. There are six straight lines in A.

11 Ludo and pontoon, brag and tennis, baseball and cricket (*1 point* if *all* correct)

12 E and L (*1 point*)
There are two alternate series. The first starts at A and advances one letter at a time: A B C D E. The second series starts at Z and goes back first two places in the alphabet (X), then three places (U), then four places (Q) and finally five places (L).

13 ADIOR (*1 point*)
The others are all anagrams of games: billards, snooker, draughts, backgammon. ADIOR is an anagram of RADIO.

96 Group 2

14 x = 37, y = 49 (*1 point* if *both* correct)
Moving clockwise from 3, the opposite number is first formed by doubling the original number and *subtracting* 1, then doubling the original number (8) and *adding* 1 (17). This procedure continues round the circle. x, therefore, is double the opposite number (19) less one (37), and y is double the opposite number (24) plus one (49).

15 The missing domino is: [· ·|· ·] (*1 point*)

Test 2

1 B (*1 point*)

2 HEAR (*2 points*)
BEAR, FEAR, TEAR and WEAR can all be used as nouns as well as verbs. HEAR can only be used as a verb.

3 Recorder, express, determine, brief, standard, tumbler, circular,, fence, hedge, bar (*2 points* if *all* correct; *1 point* if *6* correct)

4 AK, BG, CJ, DH, EI, FL (*2 points* if *all* correct)

5 $\dfrac{9}{16}$ (*1 point*)
All the other fractions contain prime numbers.

6 x = 28, y = 12, z = 540 (*2 points* if *all* correct)
The results must agree with the examples in the top row, which show that: in the first diagram all the numbers are added together and the result placed in the centre; in the second diagram the numbers in the outer square are added together and the result subtracted from the total of the numbers in the inner square (6 + 1 + 7 + 4 = 18, minus 3 + 4 + 2 + 1 = 10); in the third diagram the total of the numbers in the outer square is multiplied by the total of the numbers in the inner square (3 + 4 + 2 + 1 = 10 multiplied by 6 + 1 + 7 + 4 = 18).

Answers 97

7 FreeBOOter, hasSOCK, inVESTment, patIENt, chATter, escAPEment, rainBOW (*2 points* if *all* correct; *1 point* if 5 correct)

8 x = 243, y = 64 (*1 point* if *both* correct)
The odd numbers are trebled each time, so that 81 becomes 243. The even numbers are doubled each time, so that 32 become 64.

9 LOVE IT (*1 point*)
This is an anagram of VIOLET – a flower – whereas the others are anagrams of trees: laburnum, sycamore, chestnut.

10 x = 81, y = 432, z = 64 (*1 point* if *all* correct)
A square is worth 4, a triangle 3, a prism 27 and a cube 16. From the number 12 already inserted it is evident that the values of overlapping shapes are multiplied together.

x is a triangle overlapping a prism, hence 3 multiplied by 27 = 81; y is a prism overlapping a cube, hence 27 multiplied by 16 = 432; z is a cube overlapping a square, hence 16 multiplied by 4 = 64.

11 PAS DE DEUX (*1 point*)
This is a term used in dancing. The others are all terms used in games or sports: respectively, hockey, polo, football, tennis, and cricket.

12 CAT (*1 point*)
The words are POLECAT and TACIT.

13 JUICY (*1 point*)
Except for this one, all the words contain the name of a month *split by one letter*! Thus: CAPRIOLE, MArchY, JUNkEt.

14 13 (*2 points*)
Add together the order in the alphabet of each letter on each side of the brackets and subtract the smaller from the larger:

L = 12   E = 5   G = 7   total = 24
A = 1   R = 18   M = 13   total = 32
Difference = 8.

98 *Group 2*

    E = 5   A = 1   R = 18   total = 24
    L = 12   I = 9   P = 16   total = 37
    Difference = 13.

15 The missing domino is [3:5 domino image] and can be played at either x or y. (*1 point if* you answered *either* of these)

Test 3

1 x = 1 (*1 point*)
Columns below prime numbers add up to 10; columns below odd numbers add up to 20; columns below even numbers add up to 15.

    x is in a column below an odd number, and therefore must equal 1 in order to bring the total up to 20.

2 MRS MALAPROP (*1 point*)
Mrs Malaprop is a character in *The Rivals* by R. B. Sheridan. All the others are characters from novels by Dickens: respectively, *Barnaby Rudge, Bleak House, The Pickwick Papers, David Copperfield, Great Expectations*.

3 ORE (*1 point*)

4 £20 (*1 point*)
A 'pony' is slang for £25 and a 'monkey' is slang for £500. 'A 'pony' is 25 times a pound, and a 'monkey' is 25 times £20.

5 MELBOURNE (*1 point*)
Melbourne is *not* the capital of Australia – a distinction which belongs to Canberra. The others are the capital towns of, respectively, England, Japan, Portugal, India, France.

Answers 99

6 x = 44 (*2 points*)

Examine the *opposite* quarters of the circle. In the case of the right-hand top quarter and the left-hand bottom quarter, add the numbers in the outer ring and subtract the total of the numbers in the inner ring to give the number in the centre:

$6 + 11 + 19 + 14 = 50; 7 + 5 = 12; 50 - 12 = 38$
$3 + 9 + 16 + 17 = 45; 1 + 2 = 3; 45 - 3 = 42$

The right-hand bottom quarter indicates that you must *add* the total of the outer ring to the total of the inner ring:

$8 + 18 + 4 + 9 + 10 + 13 = 62$.

Therefore x must equal 44, being the total of all the numbers in the left-hand top quarter.

7 CAR–PEN–TER, ROT–TEN, OR–GAN, PAN–TRY, TRI–TON (*2 points* if *all* correct; *1 point* if *3* correct)

8 B (*1 point*)

9 ARTichoke, pARTition, heARTburn, thwARTing, restARted, stagpARTy, applecART (*1 point* if *all* correct)

10 1 = P, 2 = L, 3 = A, 4 = Q, 5 = U, 6 = E (*2 points* if *all* correct and entered *clockwise*; *1 point* if *all* correct, but entered *anti-clockwise*)

The letters in the three inner circles are the letters of the word in the outer circle. Thus, in the top left-hand quarter the outer ring contains the word *mocked,* and the letters in the three inner rings are: C E K O M D.

In the bottom left-hand quarter the letters in the three inner rings are: O E U L A Q, and the *only* anagram of these letters is: PLAQUE, which is inserted into the outer ring in a *clockwise* direction, to conform with the other words in the outer ring.

11 SAMOVAR (*1 point*)

A samovar is a Russian tea-making vessel. All the others are sailing vessels, respectively, Mediterranean, Arabian, Chinese and, again, Chinese.

Group 2

12 Because it prevents the diagonal line from top left to bottom right from adding to 20. (*1 point*)
All the other lines – horizontally, vertically and diagonally – add to 20.

13 21 (*1 point*)
35 squared is 1,225, which is more than 1,220. Therefore, add the largest number – 18 – to the smallest number – 3 – and the answer is 21.

14 BENEFIT (*1 point*)
The numbers on the board correspond to the alphabetic order of letters.

The first throw – 2 – lands on square 2, which represents B – the second letter in the alphabet;

the second throw – 3 – lands on square 5 to give the fifth letter of the alphabet – E;

the third throw – 5 – lands on square 10. But here there is a ladder, so that it finishes on square 14. The fourteenth letter is N;

the fourth throw brings us to 17, where there is the head of a snake, so we finish at square 5 – E again!;

the fifth throw – 1 – advances to 6, and the sixth letter of the alphabet is F;

the sixth throw – 3 – comes to square 9, and the ninth letter is I;

the final throw brings us to 15, where there is a ladder, taking us up to square 20, and the twentieth letter of the alphabet is T.

15 All the dates *ultimately* add up to four. (*2 points*)
If the digits making up the data are added together, and then the resulting digits also added together, the result is four in each case:

$$1 + 1 + 4 + 7 = 13 \quad 1 + 3 = 4$$
$$1 + 5 + 3 + 4 = 13 \quad 1 + 3 = 4$$
$$1 + 7 + 8 + 6 = 22 \quad 2 + 2 = 4$$
$$1 + 9 + 0 + 3 = 13 \quad 1 + 3 = 4$$

Test 4

1 A – 2, B – 5, C – 1 (*2 points* if *all* correct)

In A the figure rotates anti-clockwise, 45 degrees at a time. In B it rotates anti-clockwise again. Counting a move as being through 45 degrees, the first change is one move, then two moves, then three moves. Hence, the next changes should be four moves, as shown in 5.

In C the figure rotates clockwise, following the same procedure as above, and the fourth change should therefore be as shown in 1.

2 BLACK-BOX, STRAW-BERRY, OPERA-HAT, GLASS-HOUSE, MAD-CAP, SUN-DIAL, COLOUR-BLIND, CLOCK-WORK, HOME-MADE, HOUSE-MAID. (*2 points* if *all* correct; *1 point* if 7 correct)

It will be seen that several of the words in the first column can be paired with more than one word in the second column. To make the wrong choice could lead to chaos later.

Begin by examining all the words in the first column to see if there is one (or more) that can only be paired with *one* word in the second column. COLOUR immediately fulfils this, as it can only be paired with *blind*. This in turn means that BLIND cannot be paired with SUN (sunblind), so that SUN *must* be paired with DIAL. GLASS can only go with HOUSE; therefore as OPERA cannot also go with HOUSE, OPERA must be paired with HAT.

3 C (*1 point*)

C is constructed with 21 lines. All the other houses are constructed with 20 lines.

4 ALTERNATE, SOBER, ARSON (*2 points* if *all* correct)

The arrangement of the other words is as follows: ERMINE, NEUTRAL, ALSO, SOLACE, CEDAR, ARSENIC, ICED, EDUCATE, TENSION, ONAGER.

102 *Group 2*

5 TFEƧUMO (*1 point*)
The first group consists of numbers, the fifth one – 9 – being reversed.

The second group has the numbers transposed. In this case the 9 is printed correctly, but the 2 is reversed.

The third group consists of letters, which are transposed in the same way as the numbers. Just as 9 (the fifth symbol in the first group) is reversed, so is E (the fifth letter in the third group) reversed. The letter Z (the sixth letter) is reversed in the solution.

6 ELVER (*1 point*)
An elver is a young eel. The other words are names for salmon.

7 D (*1 point*)
The lines do not cross at right-angles and the line from bottom left to top right is shorter than all the other lines.

8 NEW (*2 points*)
Counting the number of strokes which make up the letters:

FIX	6 strokes
LIE	7 strokes
TAN	8 strokes
TEA	9 strokes
WET	10 strokes

To continue the sequence, the next word must be made up with 11 strokes and NEW is the only word that complies with this. (LET – 8 strokes; TIE – 7 strokes; WAY – 10 strokes; EVE – 10 strokes; WHY – 10 strokes.)

9 Surprised, desires, serif, fire-engine, enigmatic, citation (*2 points* if *all* correct)

10 C = 8, A = 5, T = 3 (*2 points* if *all* correct)
First consider C in the third line of the sum. It cannot be 0, since that is already accounted for in the second line; 1 and 2 also are accounted for. If 3 is considered, it would bring the total of the units to 8, and T would therefore be 8. The total of the tens would thus be 9,

and A in the top line would be 9. But the total of the hundreds – 9, 2 and 1 – would bring the grand total into four figures, which is wrong. C cannot be 4, since that is accounted for; if it were 5, the total of the units would be 10, making T=0, which cannot be, as 0 is already accounted for. If C were 6, T would have to be 1 (already used) and if C were 7, T would have to be 2 (again already used). 8, however, satisfies, and means that T must be 3 – provided 8 is the only valid answer for C. There is one more possibility: does C = 9? No, because, if so, the total of the units would be 14, causing T to be 4, and *that* is already accounted for.

It is now established that C is 8 and T is 3. By carrying forward 1 from the units to the tens (1 + 4 + 8 = 13), it can soon be seen that A must be 5.

11 SPATULA (*1 point*)
All the other words are names of bones.

12 ROW (*1 point*)
The words become barrow and rowan.

13 20 (*1 point*)

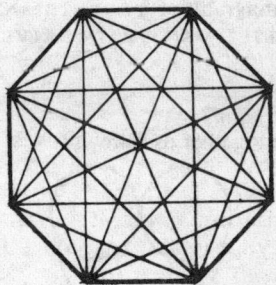

14 ACE (*2 points*)
Each letter takes its order in the alphabet – DIE = 4 9 5; CAD = 3 1 4; BEG = 2 5 7.

The totals of the columns then become: 800, 700, 600 and (the fourth column) 500.

In order to make the fourth column total 500 the word has to represent 135, which, substituted for letters, becomes A E C.

104 Group 2

15 GRIMALKIN (*1 point*)
A cat among the dogs! A grimalkin is an old she-cat, whereas all the others are breeds of dogs.

Test 5

1 RHEA (*1 point*)
The words are anagrams of fish, with the exception of RHEA, which is an anagram of hare. The fish are, respectively, trout, tuna, dace, lobster, skate.

2 IDE (*2 points*)
Two adjacent syllables in the outer ring combine with the common syllable – GER – in the centre to form words: passenGER, GERmanic, doggEREl, GERminate, manaGER, messenGER, danGERous.

That leaves only MIC, and, combined with GER, the only remaining word is 'germicide', which means that the remaining syllable is IDE.

3 SPEED TRAIN (*1 point*)
This is an anagram of PEDESTRIAN. The others are: MOTORIST, LIFT MAN, TRAIN DRIVER, PILOT, MOTOR CYCLIST.

4 B, E and F (*1 point*)
The pieces fit together as follows:

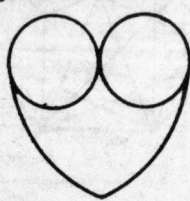

5 NF18 20 NM (*1 point*)
The first two letters of the code are dropped one place. The next number represents the order in the alphabet of the next letter in the town. The next number does likewise, and finally the last two letters in the code are raised one place.

Answers 105

6 B (*1 point*)
The word is BACTERIA.

7 MORRIS (*1 point*)
All the other words can be followed with WHEEL.

8 GO TO THE END OF THE ROAD AND TURN LEFT (*2 points*)
Start at the first letter – G. Then take the next letter – O. Miss *one*, then *two*, then *three* and then *four* letters.

After this, miss *three*, then *two*, then *one*, and then take the next letter.

This procedure is now repeated: take the next letter, then miss one, then two, and so forth. The following diagram will make this clear:

Start→	G	O	T	T	E	A	O	V
	E	T	B	A	T	H	E	R	E
	E	K	A	D	U	L	A	S	R
	F	N	A	R	N	Z	T	W	T
	G	R	R	T	■	L	I	E	H
	O	A	D	W	F	E	O	T	E
	D	D	A	I	U	Q	N	Q	S
	N	A	O	O	Z	Y	R	U	W
	L	E	S	A	E	L	O	O	H

9 10 and 80 (*1 point* if *both* correct)
There are two alternate series. The first series begins at 3 and simply advances 1 each time: 3, 4, 5, 6, 7, 8, 9, *10*. The second series multiplies the previous number first by *one*, then by *two*, then by *three*, and so on.

After 10 the next number multiplies that by 8, to become *80*.

106 Group 2

10 (*a*) Yes, on the sixth throw; (*b*) No. (*1 point* for *each* correct answer. Maximum: *2 points*)

(*a*) The throws will produce the following results:

Throw	A	B	C
1	2	4	2
2	3	6	1
3	4	1*	6
4	5	3	1*
5	6	5	6
6	1*	1	1*

* Starting at 1 after a 6 finishes on top.

(*b*) Obviously, after the sixth throw B will never reach 6. It must advance in odd numbers thereafter, showing 3, 5 and 1 recurring.

11 x = 29, y = 6 (*2 points* if *both* correct)

Consider each word in turn, starting with PET. The two numbers adjacent to P *add up* to 16, and P is the 16th letter in the alphabet. The next letter – E – is the fifth letter, and is the difference between the two adjacent numbers. The third letter – T – is the 20th letter in the alphabet, and is the sum of the 2 adjacent numbers – 10 and 10.

Following the same procedure for the next words, DOG and CAT, it then means that the letters of the word OWL are made up in the same way. Thus, x = 29 (29 less 6 = 23, and W is the 23rd letter in the alphabet and y = 6 (6 plus 6 = 12, and L is the 12th letter in the alphabet).

12 DORIC (*1 point*)

'Doric' is a type of architecture or a Greek dialect. The others are all types of window.

Answers 107

13 HOG (*2 points*)

The first number gives the first consonant of the word. *Omit the vowels*, and take the order in the alphabet of the first letter. The first number on the right of the brackets shows the vowel: A = 1, E = 2, I = 3, O = 4, U = 5. The last number again denotes the consonant in its alphabetic order, *omitting the vowels*.

Thus, 6 = H (omitting A and E); 4 = O; 5 = G (omitting A and E).

14 LUCKY (*2 points*)

The crossword grid is filled in as follows:

As the middle letter of 5 across is A and the only word that fits is TOAST, it follows that both 1 down and 3 down must end in T. As TOAST has been used, this leaves LIMIT, COMET, MERIT and YACHT.

1 down cannot be COMET, since there is no word to fit C – C – –. For a similar reason it cannot be MERIT. This means it has to be either YACHT or LUCKY. But if YACHT is chosen it means that 1 down would also have to be YACHT.

Therefore the only solution is that 1 across must be LUCKY.

Group 2

15 x = 7 (*1 point*)

Opposite quarters of the circle add up to the same number.

The top left-hand quarter contains: 3 2 4 10 7 8 6 11 1 and 5, which add up to 57; the bottom right-hand quarter contains: 10 2 6 1 3 9 10 10 4 and 2, which also add up to 57.

The top right-hand quarter contains: 7 11 8 5 3 13 9 4 9 and 1, which add up to 70; the bottom left-hand quarter contains: 6 5 13 5 9 8 7 7 and 3, which add up to 63.

Therefore, to make this up to 70, x must be 7.

Ratings

The total number of points obtainable was 100, divided as follows:

Test	Points
1	17
2	21
3	19
4	22
5	21

Knowledge, flexibility of thought and deductive reasoning accounted for 39 points.
Verbal skill accounted for 35 points.
Numerical skill accounted for 17 points.
Spatial skill accounted for 9 points.

Average score is 40 out of 100, divided as follows:

Test	Points
1	9
2	10
3	7
4	6
5	8

If you had a high score in Group One but a comparatively low score in this test it implies even more strongly that you are better at spatial skill and discrimination than in verbal skill and/or deductive thinking.

60 - 100 Excellent. The next group of tests is much more difficult, but as you have done so well so far you are on the way to getting a high overall rating even if you do not do so well in the next group.

45 - 59 Very good.

35 - 44 Around the average rating.

25 - 34 Fair.

Under 25 Poor, though if you scored well in the first test your final rating may not be too bad.

Group three
(*difficult*)

Test 1

Time limit: 60 minutes

1. What are x, y and z in this series?

    2 5 7 6 20 35 x 80 y 54 z 875 162

2. Which is the odd man out?

    OLIVE
    DOVE
    GAGE
    PIPE
    IRENE

3. What word placed in the brackets will complete the first word and start the second?

    RA(   )ROT

4. Pair words in the first column with words in the second column, finishing with ten matching pairs.

ACID	ADMIRAL
EAR	TEST
GARDEN	WIG
BLACK	BROTHER
HORSE	DROP
BIG	SHOE
WATER	HEAD
RED	SHED
SNOW	GUARD
BLOCK	MARK

114 Group 3

5 Which of the numbered figures follows H?

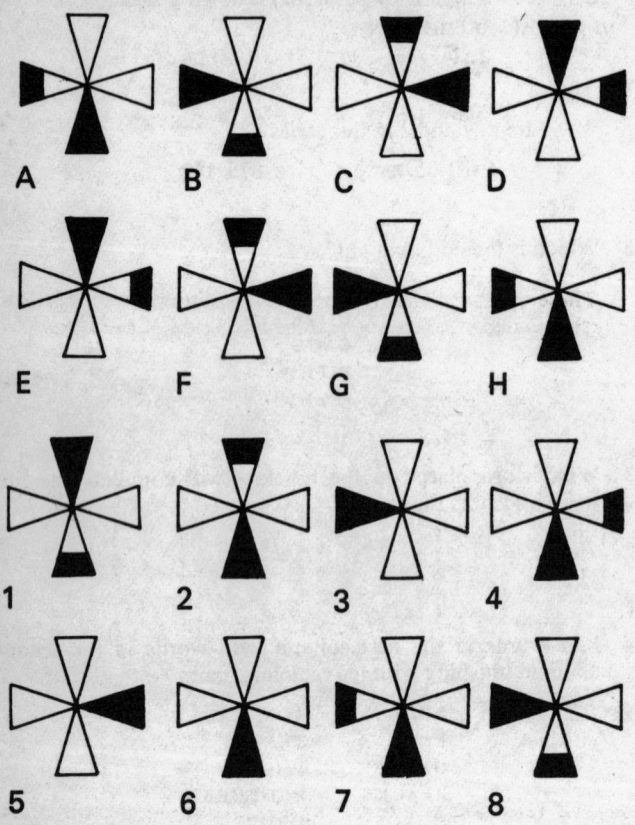

6 Which is the odd man out?

   JOULE
   OHM
   WATT
   AMPERE
   VOLT
   DYNE

Test 1 115

7 On a fruit machine there are the following symbols:

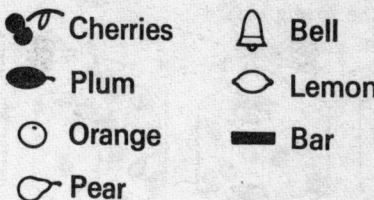

These symbols are arranged on the three reels as below (the sequence is repeated on the blind side of the reels):

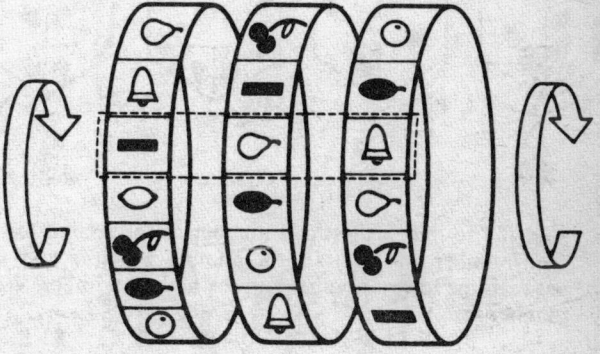

The reels rotate away from the player, in the direction shown by the arrows.

The first reel advances *four* places with each pull of the handle.

The second reel advances *two* places with each pull.

The third reel advances *one* place with each pull.

When you start playing, the symbols showing are those indicated between the dotted lines.

How many pulls must you have before there will be three of the same symbols showing between the dotted lines?

8 *One* of the faces on one of these dice cubes does not conform with the arrangement made by all the others. which is the wrong face?

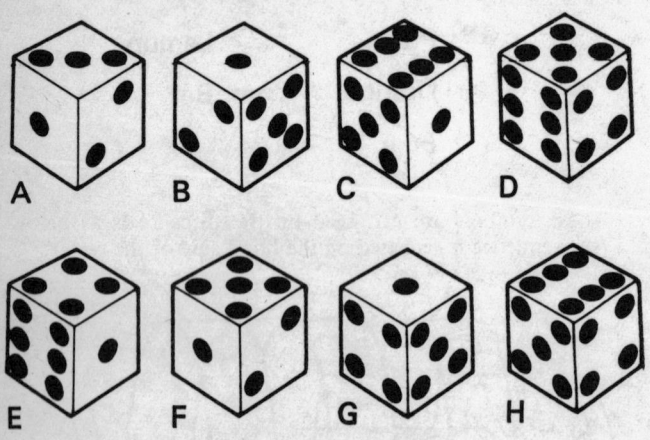

9 Add the second highest odd number to the second lowest even number and subtract the number which is mid-way between the lowest number and the highest number. What number results?

14 27 87 19 84 9 85 5 77 10 1 86 4 79 83 6 82 8

10 If LOB = ORE, what is PELT?

11 Which is the odd one out?

> PINPOINT
> WORSE
> GAELIC
> STEADFAST
> CONDEMNED
> ALMOST
> AGHAST

12 What number goes into the brackets?

   225 (159) 81
   169 (1312) 144
   441 (   ) 36

13 What are x and y?

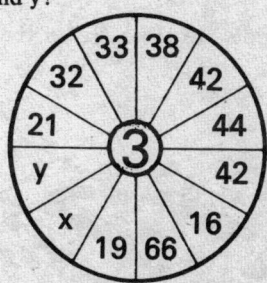

14 Which of these is wrong?

   MAN = THAT
   TAINT = EVEN
   EYE = TIME
   INN = MY
   EAT = EVIL

15 What are x and y?

Z	26
24	W
T	22
20	Q
O	19
17	L
I	x
13	y

Test 2

Time limit: 60 minutes

1. Opposite faces of a die add up to seven.
   The dice below are arranged so that all adjacent faces add up to eight.
   How many spots are there are on the blind faces – A, B, C, D and E?

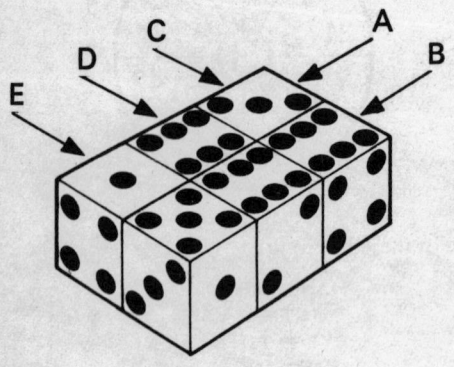

2. Which is the odd one out?

   CALLIOPE
   ERATO
   TERPSICHORE
   POLYHYMNIA
   PROCULEIUS
   MELPOMENE

3. All these were to be found in the office until they got mixed up:

   RATTY NOISE   COULD I PART?
   I SENT TO PRICE PRETTY WIRE
   RED LEGS

   Can you sort them out?

4 The two figures below rotate as follows: A rotates clockwise, first moving one face, then two, then three, and so on. If an even number faces to the front, B rotates two faces clockwise; if an odd number faces to the front B rotates three faces anti-clockwise.

At the end of five moves, what number will face to the front of B?

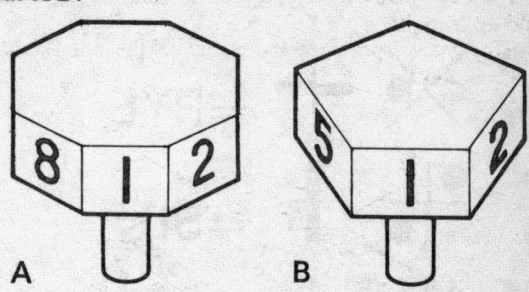

5 Which one is wrong?

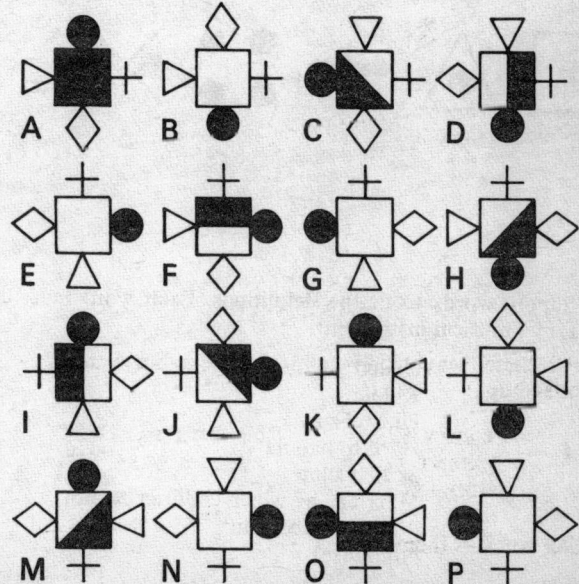

120 Group 3

6 There are *two* different words which can be placed in the brackets to end the first word and start the second word. You must give both words.

UNI(   )ER

7

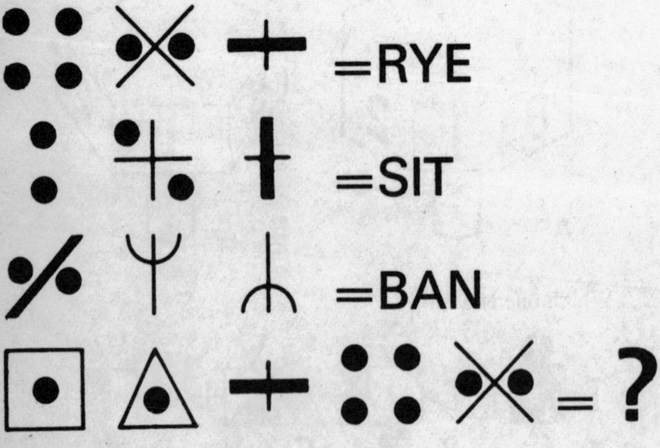

[puzzle with symbols where combinations equal RYE, SIT, BAN, and a final combination equals ?]

8 Supply words to fit the definitions. Each word must contain a musical instrument.

Coiled
Riddle
Unbroken
Hard to handle
Skilled shot
Marriage by which children cannot claim succession
Nonsense!

9 What letters complete the last line in this series?

    A B D
    D G K
    H M S
    M T B
    S B L
    — — —

10 Which is the odd man out?

    SHE STOOPS TO CONQUER
    THE APPLE CART
    THE DOCTOR'S DILEMMA
    MAJOR BARBARA
    MAN AND SUPERMAN
    PYGMALION

11 What are x and y?

    1 2 4 7 1 1 1 6 2 2 2 9 3 7 4 6 x y

12 Which is the odd man out?

    PEGASUS
    UNICORN
    CENTAUR
    GRIFFIN

13 What are x and y?

    6 J 3 D 4 G 7 C 4 J 5 x 7 y

122 Group 3

14 What are cards A, B and C?

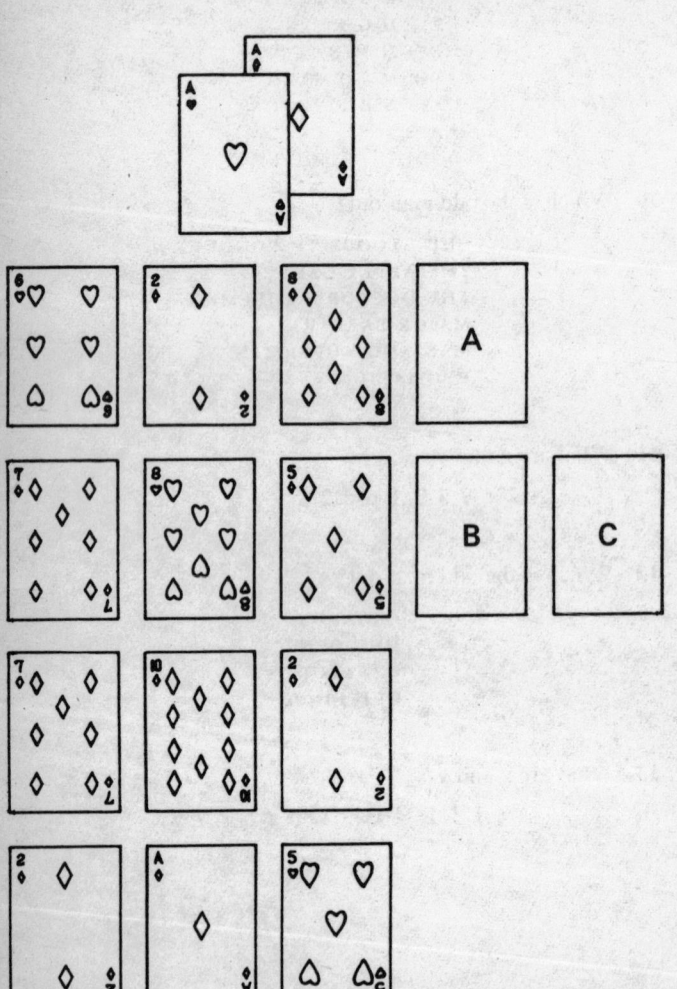

15 Pair words in the first column with words in the second column, finishing with ten pairs.

TER	STAGE
CHEESE	NATION
DASH	CAKE
BOAT	THROB
HEART	RACE
LANDING	BOARD
UP	MITE
STAG	TRAIN
CAR	BEAT
DUNDEE	PARTY

Test 3

Time limit: 65 minutes

1. Opposite sides of a die add up to seven. Assuming that odd numbers are uppermost, what is the total number of spots on the top faces of the dice shown below?

2. What is the next single digit?

   1 24 71 11 62 2 2

3. What have these words in common?

   ABRACADABRA
   SKIM
   SOME
   TRADED
   PEARL

4. If DOT = 42 and DASH = 76, what is MORSE?

5 What is the next term in this series?
(Select from the labelled figures below.)

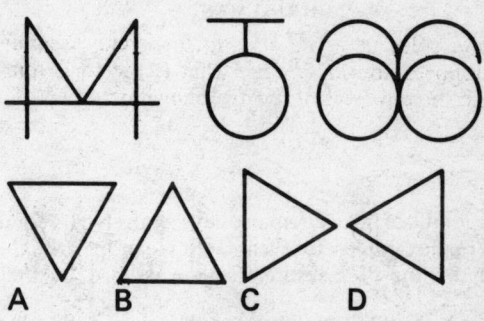

6

what is

126 Group 3

7 Which is the odd one out?

> UNDERFED
> PENNANT
> CHRISTMAS
> MOTTO
> NEBULAE
> CALLIBRATE
> FLAGON
> PROVING

8 Some units of measurement have entirely different meanings. For example, 'foot' can also mean 'part of the body'.

What units of measurement are defined by the following:

> Small island
> Respiratory organ
> Strike with the beak
> Horizontal bar
> European
> Enclosed ground
> Feline animal
> Deliver heavy blows
> Get to the bottom of
> Compact for mutual protection

9 What numbers go in the square above BRITAIN?

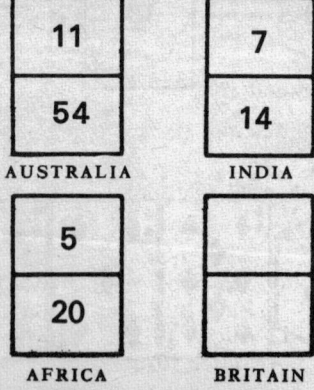

Test 3 127

10 The figures below rotates anti-clockwise. The hexagon on the top turns one face in the first move, two in the second, three in the third and four in the fourth. The square at the bottom turns through 45 degrees each time. (The faces are numbered consecutively.)

Which of the labelled figures at the bottom shows the position it will occupy after four moves?

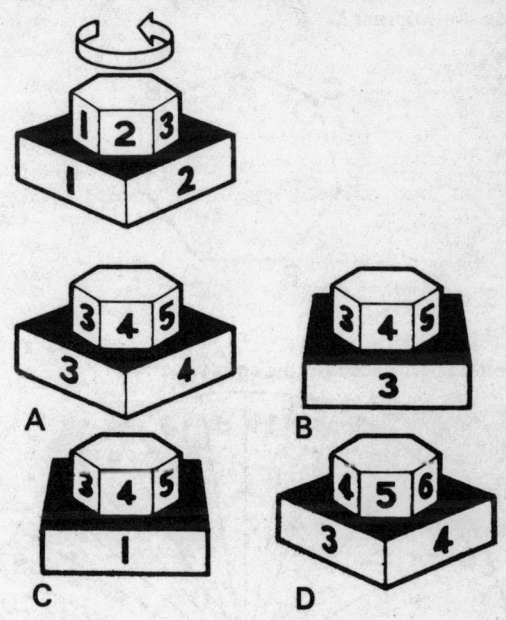

11 What are x, y and z?

3 2 5 4 4 4 4 5 6 3 6 8 2 7 x y z

12 If BEN = FIR what is CAP?

13
        3 April 1897   92
     18 September 1901   104
      6 June 1915   156
     12 August 1922   141
      4 March 1924   ?

128 Group 3

14 The black ball moves clockwise. On the first move it goes to the next corner. Then it misses one corner and goes to the next. After this it misses two corners, then three, and so forth (increasing its jump by one corner extra each time.) Meanwhile, the white ball moves anti-clockwise, one corner at a time.

How many moves will it be before both balls are in the same corner?

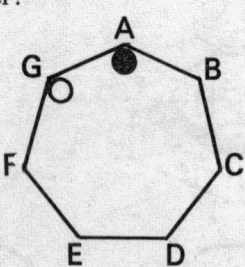

15 What letter goes into the empty sector?

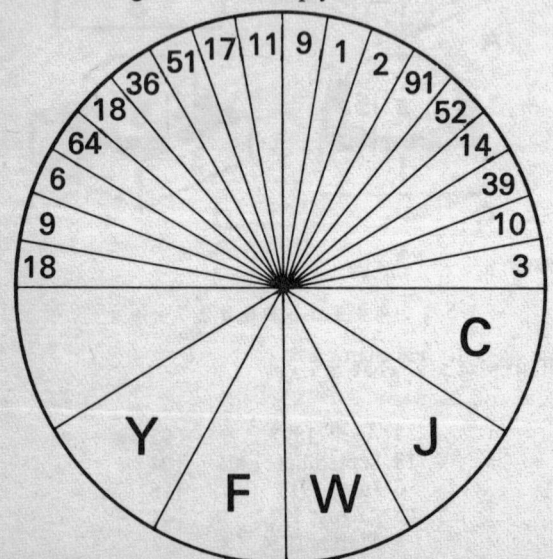

Test 4
Time limit: 75 minutes

1 When a code simply substitutes one symbol for another it is usually fairly easy to break. Can you break this code?

2 Which is the odd man out?

> EXIT
> EVIL
> ADIT
> FAKE
> ALIVE
> ACCIDENT

130 Group 3

3 Here are the reflections of six clocks as seen in a mirror. Which one is nearest to 4 o'clock?

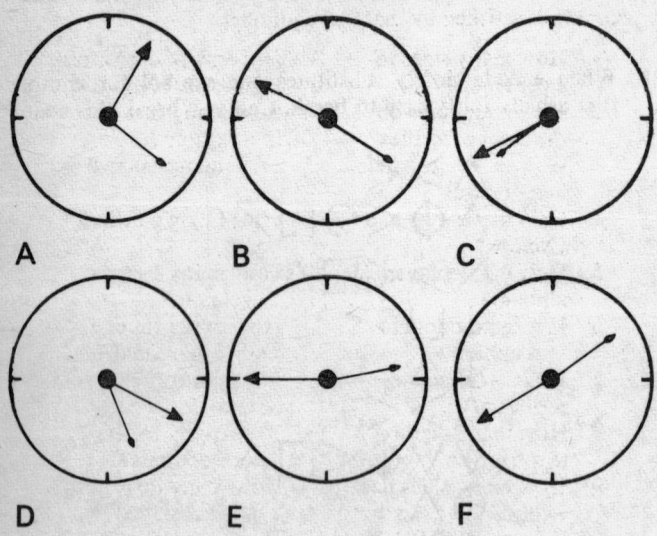

4 The first three horses in the Sullivan IQ Handicap were:

1. CALYPSO
2. GOLDEN SAM
3. HAPPY END

Which horse came fourth?

        HOT DOGS
        HONEY BEE
        BLACK KNIGHT
        ROCK SALT
        FAST RUN

5 Pair items in the first column with items in the second column. First decide what number applies to the definition in the first column and then which definition in the second column is satisfied by that same number.

1. How many sides to a pentagon?
2. How many pips on the eight of spades?
3. How many crotchets in a minim?
4. How many eyes had Cyclops?
5. How many players in a nonet?
6. How many noughts in a million?
7. What is the square root of 64?
8. How many pictures in a triptych?
9. How many sides has a rhomb?
10. How many 'pillars of wisdom'?

A. How many operas did Beethoven compose?
B. How many feet in a fathom?
C. How many muses?
D. How many cardinal points?
E. How many feet on a decapod?
F. How many times a year if 'biannual'?
G. How many 'ages of man'?
H. How many feelers has an octopus?
I. How many lines in a musical stave?
J. How many miles in a league?

6 Which is the odd one out?

ABBACY (office of an abbot)
CADGE
FAKIR
JOKUL (snow-mountain in Iceland)
LEMON
MANGO

132 Group 3

7 Arrange these figures into four pairs.

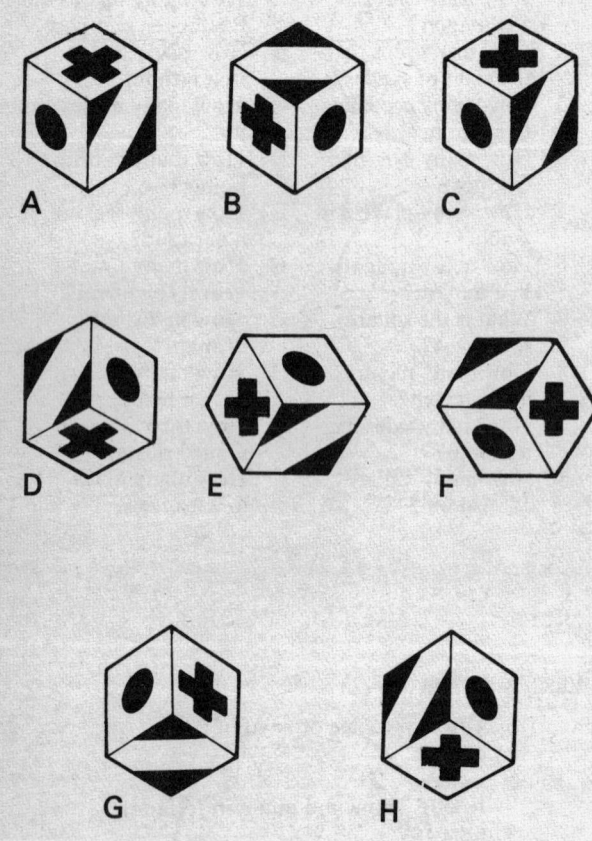

8 What are x and y?

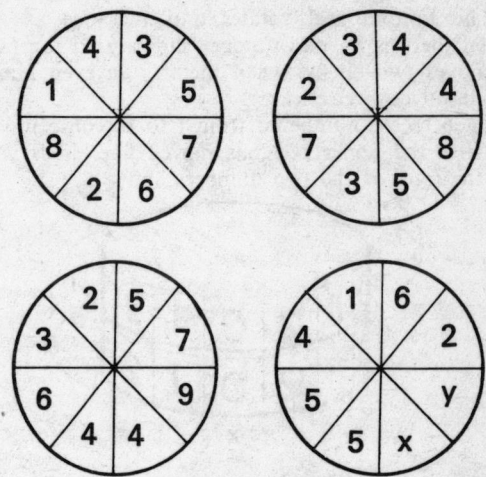

9 What words go into the brackets? Each word must link with the word before the brackets, e.g. MOUSE (TRAP) DOOR

UMBRELLA (   ) EASY (   ) CAR (   ) BLUE (   ) BONE (   ) TIME (   ) WINE (   ) HOUSE (   ) ALL (   ) ROOT (   ) WAY

10 What is x?

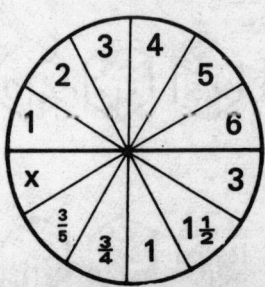

134 *Group 3*

11 The top reel rotates clockwise, one click at a time, each click bringing the next number directly above x.

The bottom reel rotates anti-clockwise as follows: when there is an odd number showing on top (above x) it moves two clicks; when there is an even number on top it moves three clicks.

Each reel is numbered from 1 to 12 consecutively.

After the upper reel has moved five clicks what will be the *total* of the two numbers above x?

12 What letters go into the brackets?

132 (L I) 108
91 (G K) 154
75 (E B) 32
68 (   ) 180

13

If 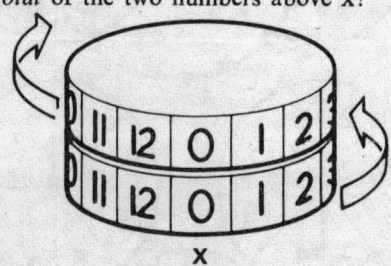 = REGION

and  = SONNET

what is

Test 4   135

14 If x is NNW, which is SE?

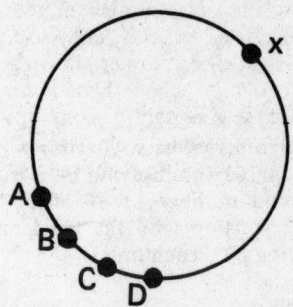

15 What time should be showing on the next clock after this series?

Answers

Test 1

1 x = 18, y = 175, z = 320 (*2 points* if *all* correct)
There are three series here. Starting with the first number: 2 6 *18* 54 162 (multiplying by 3 each time); starting with the second number: 5 20 80 *320* (multiplying by 4 each time); starting with the third number: 7 35 *175* 875 (multiplying by 5 each time).

2 GAGE (*1 point*)
'Gage' is a pledge, a challenge, or even a fruit. All the others can be associated with peace.

3 PIER (*1 point*)
The words are RAPIER and PIERROT.

4

ACID	TEST
EAR	WIG
GARDEN	SHED
BLACK	GUARD
HORSE	SHOE
BIG	BROTHER
WATER	MARK
RED	ADMIRAL
SNOW	DROP
BLOCK	HEAD

(*2 points* if *all* correct; *1 point* if 7 correct)
GARDEN can only pair with SHED and BLOCK can only pair with HEAD. This means that WATER must be paired with MARK. This eliminates pairing RED or BLACK with MARK (a weak pair, anyway), and as BLACK cannot go with HEAD it must go with GUARD. HORSE must now pair with SHOE. The only word that pairs with BROTHER is BIG, and so WIG must go with EAR. As SHOE has now been used, SNOW must go with DROP and hence ACID must pair with TEST. This leaves RED, which pairs with ADMIRAL.

Answers 137

5 7 (*1 point*)
Think of this as two independent figures mounted on a common axis. The first figure, consisting of two vanes, one completely black, rotates clockwise. The first move is a quarter-turn, then two quarter-turns, then three quarter-turns, and so on. The other figure, consisting of two vanes, one half-black, rotates anti-clockwise in the same manner.

After position H the black vane should rotate eight quarter-turns (two complete turns). The half-black vane should do the same in the opposite direction. This brings the complete figure back to the same position as shown in H.

6 DYNE (*1 point*)
This is a unit of force. The others are units of electricity.

7 22 pulls (*2 points*)
On the twenty-second pull there will be three oranges.

8 The left-hand face of D (*2 points*)
This face should be four spots and not six.
  Substitute letters for the number of spots, as follows:
  The *top* faces in the first row: 3 1 6 5 = CAFE
  The *right* faces in the first row: 2 5 1 4 = BEAD
  The *left* faces in the second row: 6 1 4 5 = FADE
  The *top* faces in the second row: 4 5 1 6 = DEAF
  The *right* faces in the second row: 1 2 5 4 = ABED
  The *left* faces in the first row: 1 2 5 6 = ABEF
ABEF is not, of course, a word, and the last letter should be changed from F to D, giving ABED. Therefore the 6 should be changed to a 4.

9 47 (*1 point*)
The second highest odd number is 85; the second lowest even number is 6; the number mid-way between 1 and 87 is 44. Therefore: 85 + 6 = 91, less 44 = 47.

10 SHOW (*2 points*)
Advance each letter three places in the alphabet.

138 Group 3

11 GAELIC (*2 points*)
All the other words contain two consecutive consonants, *ignoring vowels!* Thus: piNPoint, woRSe, steaDFast, condeMNed, aLMost, aGHast.
GAELIC contains two consecutive vowels: gAElic.

12 216 (*2 points*)
The number inside the brackets is made up with the square roots of the numbers outside the brackets:

15 squared = 225;   9 squared = 81
13 squared = 169; 12 squared = 144
21 squared = 441;   6 squared = 36.

13 x = 84, y = 22 (*2 points*)
If a number in the top half is divisible by 3 it is doubled in the opposite sector; if it is not divisible by 3 the number is halved in the opposite sector.

14 TAINT = EVEN (*2 points*)
Count the number of strokes in the letters.
    MAN (10 strokes) = THAT (10 strokes)
    EYE (11 strokes) = TIME (11 strokes)
    INN (7 strokes) = MY   (7 strokes)
    EAT (9 strokes) = EVIL (9 strokes)
But, TAINT (11 strokes) does not equal EVEN (13 strokes).

15 x = 15, y = F (*1 point for each. Maximum 2 points*)
In the top line, Z is the twenty-sixth letter, as shown. In the second line, 24 indicates X, which is dropped one place to give W. In the third line, 22 indicates V, which is dropped two places to give T. In the third line, 20 indicates T, which is dropped three places to give Q, and so on.

Applying this same procedure in the seventh line, the letter I is the ninth letter and must be raised six places to give 15. In the last line, the thirteenth letter is M, which must be dropped seven places to give F.

Test 2

1 A = 1, B = 2, C = 2, D = 4, E = 5 (*1 point* if *all* correct)

2 PROCULEIUS (*1 point*)
He is a character in *Anthony and Cleopatra*. All the other words are names of muses.

3 STATIONERY, RECEPTIONIST, LEDGERS, DUPLICATOR, TYPEWRITER (*1 point* if *all* correct)

4 1 (*1 point*)

	A	B
First move	2	3
Second move	4	5
Third move	7	2
Fourth move	3	4
Fifth move	8	1

5 M (*2 points*)
The figures are established in the top line, thereafter being turned in various directions. The half-shaded square is shown in C, and if that is turned so that the cross is at the bottom it will be seen that the square is half-shaded in the top left-hand section, whereas that in M is half-shaded in the bottom right-hand section.

6 FORM and CORN (*2 points* if *both* correct)
The words thus become UNIFORM and FORMER; UNICORN and CORNER.

7 QUERY (*2 points*)
Here it is obvious that symbols have been substituted for letters. The symbols representing the first two letters of the final five-lettered word have not been used previously, but by comparing the last three symbols it is clear that they are derived from the letters ERY, as shown in the first word.

What we are looking for, therefore, is a five-lettered word ending in ERY. The only words that fit this are: FIERY, BEERY, EVERY and EMERY. But it cannot be

FIERY, as the I has already appeared in SIT. It cannot be BEERY as both B and E have already been used (SIT and RYE). It cannot be either EVERY or EMERY since E has been used in RYE. The only word in which symbols have not already been used for the first two letters is QUERY.

8 ConvoLUTEd, conunDRUM, invIOLAte, tHORNY, sHARPshooter, mORGANatic, FIDDLEsticks! (*2 points* if *all* correct; *1 point* if 5 correct)

9 Z K W (*2 points* if *all* correct)
Moving across from top to bottom, the letters advance one place followed by two places followed by three, and so on. Thus, in the top line A advances first to B and then B advances two places to D.

Moving vertically down the left-hand column, the letters advance three places, then four, then five, and so on.

Therefore the last letter in the left-hand vertical column must be Z (seven places from S). The letters on the right of Z must be K (advanced eleven places from Z, starting again at A), and W (advancing twelve).

10 SHE STOOPS TO CONQUER (*1 point*)
This is the title of a play by Oliver Goldsmith, whereas all the other plays were written by G. B. Shaw.

11 x = 5, y = 6 (*2 points*)
There are no spaces between the numbers, but if they are spaced correctly they appear like this:

1 2 4 7 11 16 22 29 37 46 xy

It is then evident that the series advances progressively by 1, 2, 3, 4 etc. Thus the last number shown – 46 – should advance ten places to 56.

12 GRIFFIN (*1 point*)
A griffin is a fabulous creature with an eagle's head and wings and the body of a lion. The others are types of mythical horses: Pegasus was a winged horse; a unicorn was a fabulous horse with a horn; a centaur was a horse with a human body.

Answers 141

13 x = F, y = K (*2 points* if *both* correct)

An even number before a letter drops that letter that number of places in the alphabet when the next letter appears; an odd number before a letter advances that letter by that number of places in the alphabet when a letter next appears.

Thus J is dropped six places to D; D is raised three places to G; G is dropped four places to C; C is raised seven places to J; J is dropped four places to F, and F (which we have now established) is raised five places to K.

14 A = R, B = E, C = E (*2 points* if *all* correct)

There are 26 letters in the alphabet and 26 cards in two suits. The two suits at the top indicate the order of the letters – the ace of hearts is the first letter (A) and the ace of diamonds is the fourteenth letter (N).

Substituting letters for the cards, the first line becomes: FOU–; the second line: THR– –; the third line: TWO; the fourth line: ONE. Obviously, therefore, the first line spells FOUR and the second line spells THREE.

15
TER	RACE
CHEESE	MITE
DASH	BOARD
BOAT	TRAIN
HEART	THROB
LANDING	STAGE
UP	BEAT
STAG	PARTY
CAR	NATION
DUNDEE	CAKE

(*2 points* if *all* correct; *1 point* if 7 correct)

First look for words which can only be paired with one other word. DASH only goes with BOARD; CAR only goes with NATION; DUNDEE only goes with CAKE. STAG must go with PARTY, since it cannot now go with NATION, and therefore LANDING (which cannot now pair with PARTY) must pair with STAGE.

If BOAT went with RACE, TER would have to go with MITE, and as this would only leave BOARD to go with CHEESE (and BOARD has already been used) it follows that BOAT must pair with TRAIN. This in turn means that UP cannot pair with TRAIN and must therefore go with BEAT (STAGE has already been used). HEART cannot go with BEAT, and so must be paired with THROB. Finally, CHEESE must now pair with MITE and TER with RACE.

Test 3

1 24 (*1 point*)

The first die must have five spots on the top, since the other odd numbers are already shown.

The second die (in the top line) has one spot opposite the 6 and 5 opposite the 2, which means the top face must show 3 spots.

The third has a 1 opposite the 6, which means, as the 3 is already shown, that 5 must be on top. The fourth die (first in the bottom line) has a 3 opposite the 4 and must have 5 on top.

The fifth already shows a 1 and a 5, so must have a 3 on top.

The last one must have a 1 opposite the 6 and, with 5 already showing, a 3 on top.

Summing up, the top faces are: 5 3 5 5 3 3 = 24.

2 9 (*2 points*)

The spacing must be changed as follows:
             1 2 4 7 11 16 22 29
showing a series that increases progressively by 1, 2, 3, 4, 5, 6 and 7.

3 If the letters are given their respective order in the alphabet, they each total 52 (*2 points*)

Answers 143

For example:

    A = 1
    B = 2
    R = 18
    A = 1
    C = 3
    A = 1
    D = 4
    A = 1
    B = 2
    R = 18
    A = 1
         ──
         52
         ──

4 65 (*2 points*)

Each letter takes the value of its *reverse* order in the alphabet, thus:

    M = 14 (reversed in alphabet)
    O = 12
    R = 9
    S = 8
    E = 22
        ──
        65
        ──

5 A (*2 points*)

The symbols in the top line are made up with the numbers 4, 5 and 6. In each case the number is printed first backwards and then forwards, joined to each other.

Therefore the next term consists of number 7, first backwards and then forwards, joined together, thus:

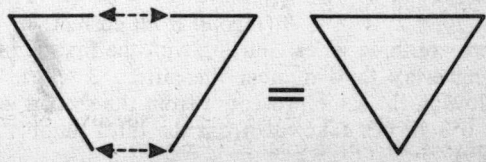

144 *Group 3*

6 POTHERB (*2 points*)
The spots on the dice represent the letters T, O and P. One spot is T, two spots are O and three spots are P (see die on top).

There are 26 cards in the two suits, and each card represents a letter in the alphabet, the ace of spades being A (first letter) and the king of clubs being Z (twenty-sixth letter). This is clear from the fact that AZ completes the first word.

Therefore, in the second line, beginning with P O T, we have the eight of spades (H = eighth letter), five of spades (E = fifth letter), five of clubs (R = eighteenth letter) and two of spades (B = second letter).

7 PENNANT (*1 point*)
All the other words contain a boy's name *in reverse*, thus: unDERfed, christMAS, MOTto, NEBulae, caLLIBrate, FLAgon, pROVing. PENNAnt contains a *girl's* name in reverse.

8 Inch, gill, peck, perch, pole, yard, ounce, pound, fathom, league (*2 points* if *all* correct; *1 point* if 7 correct)

9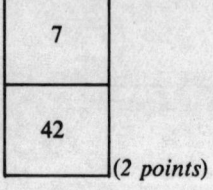
(*2 points*)

The top squares contain the total of the value of the vowels: A = 1, E = 2, I = 3, O = 4 and U = 5. The bottom squares contain the total value of the consonants in their alphabetic order, *omitting the vowels*.

10 A (*2 points*)

11 x = 10, y = 1, z = 8 (*1 point* if *all* correct)
There are three series. Starting with the first number and taking every third number thereafter: 3 4 5 6 7 *8* (z). Following the same procedure from the second number: 2 4 6 8 *10* (x). Likewise from the third number: 5 4 3 2 *1* (y).

12 GET (*1 point*)
Advance each letter four places.

13 63 (*2 points*)
The number beside the first date gives the number of days already gone in that year. The number beside the second date gives the number of days remaining in that year.

This procedure is repeated, so that for 4 March 1924 you must give the number of days already gone in that year. But, remember, it was a *leap year*!

14 5 (*1 point*)
At the end of five moves both balls will be in corner B.

15 Z (*1 point*)
Consider the three sectors opposite each letter. Subtract the sum of the two lower numbers from the higher number to give the order in the alphabet of the letter. Thus, opposite C, 6 + 9 = 15. 18 − 15 = 3, that is, the third letter of the alphabet.

Test 4

1 THE TREASURE CHEST IS IN THE FOREST AT THE SECOND TREE (*2 points* if *all* correct)
As T and E are the most commonly used letters, and noticing that this combination of symbols occurs no fewer than three times:

$$\wedge > <$$

it is a reasonable inference that it is the definite article.

Substituting these letters where they occur elsewhere we have:
THE T-E----E -HE T   THE   E T T THE
-E---- T-EE.

The only words that fit the last word are TREE or THEE, and since it cannot be THEE (H has been accounted for) the symbol for R is now known, making the second word TRE----RE. Now observe the two 2-lettered words, both beginning with the same letter. By elimination it can be inferred that these words are IN, IS or IT. Since IT can be ruled out (T has been established), the words are almost certainly IS and IN, with the first letter almost assuredly I. Substituting both possibilities of N or S in the third word of the message we get: –HENT or –HEST. Obviously this word must be CHEST, and the third letter of the tenth word is C, giving us: SEC–N–. We now have the following:

THE TRE–S–RE CHEST IS IN THE ––REST –T THE SEC–N–D TREE.

The rest now falls into place. The eighth word must be AT, since it cannot be IT (I is already accounted for) and the second word is TREAS–RE (obviously TREASURE). The seventh word is ––REST and the tenth word SEC–N–. This latter word must be SECOND, supplying the O in the other word: –OREST. The only possibility here is FOREST, and the message can be completed.

You may have proceeded in a different way, as this is only a suggested method of breaking the code.

2 FAKE (*1 point*)
All the others contain Roman figures: exIt, evIl, aDIt, aLIve, accIdent.

3 C (*2 points*)
The clocks acutally show the following times:

A	7.55
B	8.10
C	4.20
D	6.40
E	9.15
F	10.20

Did you think of holding the page up to the light and looking at them from the other side?

4 HOT DOGS (*2 points*)
The winner has a value of 91 (add the order in the alphabet of all the letters: C = 3, A = 1, L = 12, Y = 25, P = 16, S = 19, O = 15). The second has a letter-value of 90. The third has a letter-value of 89.

Therefore the fourth horse must have a letter-value of 88, and the only horse to satisfy this condition is HOT DOGS.

Answers 147

5 1 — I, 2 — E, 3 — F, 4 — A, 5 — C, 6 — B, 7 — H, 8 — J, 9 — D, 10 — G (*2 points* if *all* correct; *1 point* if 7 correct)

6 FAKIR (*2 points*)
The other words contain three *consecutive* letters spaced alternatively: ABBaCy, CADgE, JOKuL, LEMoN, MANgO.

7 A D, B G, E F, C H (*1 point* if *all* correct)

8 x = 10, y = 3 (*2 points*)
Comparing the relevant sectors with previous ones, you will find that previous numbers in the sector occupied by x are 7, 8 and 9; in the case of the sector occupied by y the preceding numbers are 6, 5 and 4.

9 STAND, STREET, BOY, WHALE, MEAL, TABLE, GLASS, HOLD, SQUARE, CAUSE (*2 points* if *all* correct; *1 point* if 7 correct)
The linked words are:
UMBRELLA STAND, STAND EASY, EASY STREET, STREET CAR, CARBOY, BOY BLUE, BLUE WHALE, WHALEBONE, BONE MEAL, MEAL-TIME, TIME TABLE, TABLE WINE, WINE GLASS, GLASS HOUSE, HOUSEHOLD, HOLDALL, ALL SQUARE, SQUARE ROOT, ROOT CAUSE, CAUSEWAY.

10 x = ½ (*2 points*)
Numbers in the lower half are the reciprocals of those in the opposite sectors multiplied by three. Thus, 3 (in the lower half) is 1/1 multiplied by 3 = 3; 1½ is ½ multiplied by 3 = 1½.

11 6 (*1 point*)
5 on the upper reel and 1 on the lower reel.

12 D J (*3 points*)
In the first line 132 is 12 times *11* and 108 is 9 times *12*. In the brackets we find L (the twelfth letter) and I (the ninth letter).
In the second line 91 is 7 times *13* and 154 is 11 times *14*. In the brackets are G (the seventh letter) and K (the eleventh letter).

148 *Group 3*

In the third line 75 is 5 times *15* and 32 is twice *16*. In the brackets are E – the fifth letter – and B – the second letter.

In the last line 68 is 4 times *17* and 180 is 10 times *18*, and so the letters are D (the fourth letter) and J (the tenth letter).

A tough one, this.

13 BOUGHT (*2 points*)
Advance each letter by the number of spots on the face of the die that precedes it. In the top line, 1 on the die advances the Q to R; 2, on the next face, advances the C two places to E; 4 on the next face advances C to G; 6 on the next face advances C to I; 5 on the next face advances J to O; 3 on the next face advances K to N.

14 C (*1 point*)
NNW is mid-way between north-west and north. C is mid-way between south and east.

15 8.29 (*2 points*)
The previous clocks register the following times: 1.23, 2.34, 3.45, 4.56, 6.07 (*that is* 5.67!), 7.18 (*that is* 6.78!). Therefore the next clock must register 7.89 (*that is* 8.29!).

Ratings

The total number of points obtainable was 100, divided as follows:

Test	Points
1	25
2	24
3	24
4	27

These tests were very difficult, most points being obtained from deductive reasoning and flexibility of thought, which accounted for 66% of the points.
Verbal skill accounted for 14 points.
Numerical skill accounted for 16 points.
Spatial skill accounted for only 4 points.

Average score is as low as 28 points, divided as follows:

Test	Points
1	8
2	8
3	5
4	7

A very low mark in this group combined with a relatively high mark in Group One implies that you are far better at spatial questions than those demanding deductive reasoning. High marks in this group and in Group Two combined with relatively low marks in Group One probably means that you are better at deductive reasoning and flexibility of thought than in problems calling for spatial skill.

23 – 32 You can rate yourself as about average at these very difficult tests.
33 – 49 Very good.
50 – 65 Excellent.
Over 65 Genius class!

Group 3

Under 23 If you rated fairly well in the previous tests don't be downhearted. If under 15, combined with low scores in the previous tests I would suggest that you have more practice at these types of tests. Perhaps you are unfamiliar with them, anyway, and had difficulty in understanding how to tackle them.

Final Ratings
Based on all the tests

There were 100 points obtainable in each group, so the total number of points obtainable was 300.

The subjects were divided approximately as follows:

	Points	%
Deductive reasoning, flexibilty of thought and a small amount of knowledge	119	40
Verbal skill	78	26
Numerical skill	53	18
Spatial skill	50	16

The average score is 118 points.

225 – 300 So extraordinarily good that you must have found the book too easy! Your intelligence rating is of the highest degree and you should do well in all tests of this nature.

160 – 224 Excellent.

130 – 159 Very good.

110 – 129 Around average.

95 – 109 Fair.

Under 95 Poor, but keep persevering with these types of tests and you will improve as you become more familiar with them. At any rate, I hope you have enjoyed trying them and have had some benefit from them.

Space for Notes

Space for Notes

Space for Notes

Space for Notes

Space for Notes

Space for Notes

Space for Notes